Energize Your Life

DEL MILLERS, PhD

Also By Del Millers

**Fitness & Spirituality
Dr. Del's 10-Minute Meals
Dr. Del's Rapid Fatloss Program**

**Meet Dr. Del online and receive free coaching at
www.drdelmillers.com**

Energize Your Life!

Activate the 7 Pillars of Positive Energy that Make You Feel Alive!

Del Millers, PhD

Energize Your Life
Activate the Seven Pillars of Positive Energy that Make You Feel Alive.

Del Millers, Ph.D.

Published by

Spiritwind Publications
Playa Vista, CA 90094 U.S.A.
818-293-7335

All rights reserved. No part of this book may be reproduced or transmitted in any form or by any means, electronic or mechanical, including photocopying, recording or by any information storage and retrieval system without written permission from the author, except for the inclusion of brief quotations in a review.

Library of Congress Control Number: 2015914993

Publisher's Cataloging-in-Publication Data

Millers, Del.

Energize your life : activate the 7 pillars of positive energy that make you feel alive / Del Millers.

pages cm
ISBN: 978-0-9856443-8-3 (pbk.)

1. Self-actualization (Psychology) 2. Energy psychology. 3. Motivation (Psychology) 4. Interpersonal relations. 5. Quality of life. I. Title.

BF637.S8 M55 2015
650.1—dc23

2015914993

Design by Linda B
Author Photo by Michael Burr Photography

Printed in the United States of America

"Walk as if you are kissing the Earth with your feet."
– Thich Nhat Hahn

Energize Your Life

For my four angels: Jill, Novi, Zolie and Saphira

Contents

Introduction: A New Way to Live and Work

Chapter 1: The Energized Life - *page 7*
- The Seven Pillars of Positive Energy

Chapter 2: Pillar #1: Ignite Your Passions…Fuel Your Purpose - *page 21*
- The Passion Manifesto: Uncovering Your Passions
- The Passion Manifesto: Seven Keys to Uncovering Your Passions
- Love It or Leave It: Creating Fulfilling Work
- Before You Ditch Your Day Job.
- Passion-Purpose Action Plan

Chapter 3: Pillar #2: Accelerate Your Personal Evolution - *page 49*
- 7 Ways to Expand Your Self-Awareness
- Personal Evolution Action Plan

Chapter 4: Pillar #3: Cultivate Physical Vitality - *page 67*
- 7 Ways to Cultivate Physical Vitality
- Physical Vitality Action Plan

Chapter 5: Pillar #4: Become a Conduit for Positive Energy - *page 85*
- 7 Ways to Cultivate Positive Energy Everyday
- Positive Energy Action Plan

Chapter 6: Pillar #5: Practice Positive Psychology - *page 95*
- 7 Simple Brain Hacks for Increasing Your Positive Energy
- Positive Psychology Action Plan

Chapter 7: Pillar #6: Increase Your Prosocial Behavior - *page 125*
- Giving and the Brain—The "Helper's High"
- Altruism in the Workplace
- 7 Ways to Increase Your Positive Energy through Simple Acts of Kindness
- Prosocial Behavior Action Plan

Chapter 8: Pillar #7: Give Yourself Permission to Play - *page 133*
- The Science of Play
- Play and On The Job Productivity
- 7 Ways to Increase Your Positive Energy through Play
- Play Action Plan

Closing Note: Every Energy Reaction Needs a Catalyst, What's Yours?

Energize Your Life Tools & Resources
- About the Author
- Essential Reading

The 7 Pillars of Positive Energy

1. Ignite Your Passions…Fuel Your Purpose
Passion energizes. Purpose motivates.

2. Accelerate Your Personal Evolution
Self-awareness leads to emotional maturity, which frees us to respond differently.

3. Cultivate Physical Vitality
Physical vitality expands our energy capacity.

4. Become a Conduit for Positive Energy
Positive energy attracts. Negative energy repels.

5. Practice Positive Psychology
Positive thoughts and emotions program the brain (and our subconscious) for positive action.

6. Increase Your "Prosocial Behavior"
Simple acts of kindness, good for the doer too.

7. Give Yourself Permission to Play
Play increases our capacity to respond appropriately to the unexpected.

Introduction: A New Way to Live and Work

"We all have two lives. The second one starts when we realize that we only have one."
— Tom Hiddleston

America is experiencing a personal energy crisis.

Most of us live very stressful and chaotic lives. In fact, we are so busy that we hardly have time to sit and enjoy a meal with our families anymore.

This way of living is killing us, whether we choose to acknowledge it or not. But, the data doesn't lie. Today, we're experiencing more stress and lifestyle-related diseases than ever before.

We fool ourselves into thinking that our personal health challenges are the result of bad genes. But the truth is it is our poor lifestyle habits that activate expression of those genes.

The way we live — including the way we work — not only robs us of our health and puts a strain on time and energy resources, it blocks our access to our most essential sources of energy, leaving us feeling physically, mentally, and emotionally drained.

Introduction

Growing up in New York City, watching television reruns of CHiPs, Charlie's Angels, and Starsky & Hutch, I dreamt about the year-round summers and beautiful beaches in Los Angeles. So, imagine my delight, when in 1990 I graduated from Columbia University with a degree in Electrical Engineering and had a job offer in Los Angeles!

I was very excited to leave the congested city life and cold winters behind.

My excitement, however, was short-lived. Working 10-12 hour days left me perpetually exhausted. I had to get up at five AM just to get my workout done, which meant getting less than six hours of sleep each night.

Working such long hours also meant not having time for friends or much of a social life. Worst of all, I developed the bad habit of eating out all the time in an area with few healthy options.

I was unhappy. I felt drained every night. I was unfulfilled. My new job was literally, bad for my health. This lasted for two years before I finally asked myself the same question I now ask my consulting clients: "why are you doing this to yourself?"

After four years in corporate America, I made the discovery that I am not the employee type. So, I hung up my suit and tie and bid farewell to corporate America to pursue the uncertain life of an entrepreneur.

My experience working in corporate America is not all that uncommon, however. Most people respond to rising work demands by putting in more time. They stay late at the office and still take work home. Sound familiar?

Rising demands on our time eventually takes a toll on health, energy, and the very experience of living.

But it doesn't have to be that way. The old paradigm of sacrificing health, family time and quality of life so that we can get more done is yesterday's thinking.

Fortunately, more and more of us are realizing that the way we currently live is unsustainable. We recognize that time may be a limited commodity, but energy is renewable and therefore limitless.

The new way to live is to cultivate positive energy in all areas. This in turn will make your life — including your work — more engaging, fulfilling and definitely more meaningful.

By focusing on your energy needs, you can actually get more done, make a difference — and still have time for the things that matter most. This realization has completely transformed my life — and the lives of many of my clients who have made dramatic changes as well. It wasn't easy, but most are happier, healthier, and more fulfilled in all aspects of their lives than before.

This is possible for you too.

Introduction

When you learn how to activate the seven pillars of positive energy, you will definitely achieve a higher level of mastery over your life.

Mastery is achieved by having a growth mindset. This means being willing to change how you interpret your experiences, in addition to developing new positive psychology skills to successfully deal with life's adversities.

The seven pillars of positive energy that are outlined in this book will help you reclaim control of your life. You will be challenged to develop greater awareness of how and why you live the way that you do.

Why do you do the work that you do? Is it fulfilling? Can you make it more fulfilling? Can you generate more passion and purpose?

The truth is, if your work doesn't energize you, it is a major "energy sucker."

Secondly, are you growing, changing, evolving, or are you remaining stagnant? In other words, are you working toward your own personal evolution?

To evolve is to develop a greater awareness of self and the world around you.

Finally, there have been many books written on how to cultivate positive energy. However, none have touched on how to activate all seven sources of positive energy — passion and purpose, personal evolution, physical vitality, positive energy, positive psychology, prosocial behavior, and play.

Each of us has access to all seven sources of positive energy. However, specific action is required to activate each pillar as a source of positive energy. Without awareness and action, these vital sources often become major "energy suckers" instead.

Energize Your Life shows you how to activate these seven sources. Each of them has the potential to inject massive amounts of positive energy into your work, personal life, and relationships.

So, what happens when we inject positive energy into our work, our family lives, or the pursuit of our dreams? We experience massive breakthroughs because positive energy programs the brain — and the subconscious — for productive, beneficial action.

My hope is that after reading this book you will be inspired to develop a personal action plan to liberate yourself from the culture of overwork that is preventing you from fully living; rediscover what truly drives you; give yourself permission to play and claim your "joy moments" every day.

Read on.

1

The Energized Life

"Without energy, life is merely a latent possibility.
The world belongs to the energetic."
– Ralph Waldo Emerson

Energy is the source of ALL life. It is the life force of nature.

The simplistic definition of energy is that it is the capacity to do work. Not just physical work, but mental, emotional and spiritual work too.

However, a more sophisticated definition could be: energy is the vehicle that allows life to multiply itself and find its *fullest expression.*

In the beginning, the universe was all energy. Then, that energy changed into energized particles or matter. The stars, planets, and the millions of organisms that inhabit the earth, as we know it, are all energized particles.

These organisms didn't just show up on the earth, they evolved from simple organisms to more complex ones.

And so here we are; *the most advanced species* that we know of on this planet — human beings. We are the direct result of life striving for its fullest expression.

So isn't it clear that the single most important purpose of your life and mine is to live? *To live fully, enthusiastically and vibrantly.*

To multiply our lives, not just in the sense of procreation, but to *maximize our fullest potential* as intelligent beings.

To continue the process of *personal evolution*. To make *more of it* during the relatively short lifespan between birth and death. Before our life energy is returned to the "collective free energy" source, we are charged with being the vehicles through which life finds its *fullest expression.*

This, I believe, is the purpose of our lives.
To put it bluntly, if you're constantly feeling tired, lethargic, unmotivated and uninspired, you're not living the life you were meant to live.

To multiply your life is to live with passion and purpose...
- To live in such a way that inspires you and those around you.
- To co-create something that is bigger than you.

Here's the bottom line (and the ambition of this book): To make a contribution to the world you must learn how to utilize more of the "collective free energy" — thus turning it into something that first inspires you and then those whose paths are brightened by your light.

And I have good news: you already possess the capacity to activate the essential dimensions of energy and to start living the powerful, energized life you were meant to live!

I hope this book will serve as a roadmap for your quest to energize your life and I am happy to be your guide. What qualifies me to be your guide? Well, I've been a student and seeker of this way of living practically my entire life.

As I've said before, to live an energized life is to live a life that inspires you and those whose path is brightened by your light.

I'm honored and humbled that throughout my life I have had the pleasure and privilege of inspiring others all over the world to live better lives. Inspired lives.

Lives in the pursuit of freedom, fulfillment and fun.

Lives bold enough to unchain the adventurous spirit of those who dare to aspire for more than title and status.

Lives in pursuit of passion, purpose and personal evolution.

Twenty years ago, I walked away from corporate America because it was sucking the life out of me. I needed room to breathe. To explore. To create an inspired life.

Don't get me wrong. I am not saying that you have to quit your job, as I did. However, you do have to be honest with yourself and either find ways to *love what you do* or make a plan to *leave it behind*.

In short, to live an energized life, you either have to learn to love your job or leave it.

If you're sitting somewhere in between, as so many of the masses are, you will become enslaved by boredom and bureaucracy. Ultimately, you will end up as nothing more than a fragment of yourself.

You deserve more.

You deserve to find or create work that allows you to thrive and feel fully alive.

You deserve to answer with a resounding "NO!" to that little voice that keeps whispering in your ears, "is this all there is?"

You deserve nothing less than to live inspired with passion and purpose, because only then will you live vibrantly, love passionately, and unwrap the gift of the energized life.

I often sit and marvel at my three young daughters. How is it they're able to run around energetically from the minute they awake until well past their bedtime?

The answer came to me as I watched them play.

They are completely lost in the moment. To them the only thing that matters is what's happening now, not what happened five minutes ago or what's going to happen in the future.

They never lack energy because they live in the moment.

In a single day, they have experienced every known emotional state and are able to awaken the next day refreshed, and ready to do it all again without being burdened by what happened yesterday.

To energize your life, you must not only live with passion and purpose, but you must also learn to unshackle yourself from the baggage of the past and the anxiety of the future. Both are major "energy suckers."

To learn to live in the present and to celebrate life with the enthusiasm of a four-year-old is the art of living an energized life.

Too often, the way we live and work robs us of our passion, purpose and opportunities for personal evolution — it drains our positive energy.

Most of us are exhausted when we go to sleep at night and still tired when we awake.

We're constantly on the go trying our best to "get it all done" within the limited amount of time that we have. Even taking a real lunch break is a luxury we cannot afford because we have to keep plugging along.

We lack physical vitality because we neglect our own self-care, quality time with family and friends — and too often, we can't even remember why we're running ourselves right into our own graves, literally.

So, we turn to energy drinks, caffeine and other artificial stimulants for quick jolts that in turn, leave us even more depleted, disengaged, and with more stress-related disorders.

The way we're living — and working — is unsustainable and we know it.

Fortunately, the tides are turning. We're waking up. We're asking ourselves WHY? Why am I doing this to myself? Why am I doing this to my family? Why am I doing this with the one precious life that I've been given?

Why am I spending my time digging my own grave instead of, as Thoreau put it, striving to "suck out all the marrow of life?"

Over the past twenty years, I have consulted with thousands of clients (doctors, lawyers, business executives, athletes, office workers, and stay-at-home moms), who all had one thing in common:

They all had an epiphany that the way they were living their lives was stealing their joy, robbing them of vital energy, and leaving them feeling unfulfilled. They were all tired, drained, and overcommitted and wanted to feel alive again.

What they discovered, and hopefully you will too, is that to energize your life is to learn how to renew your energy capacity when it is depleted and to re-discover what drives you.

It is to find fulfillment in your daily activities and to liberate yourself from whatever is holding you back from living.

It is to unchain your adventurous spirit from the culture of overwork and to pursue your passions.

To energize your life is to come alive!

Are you ready?

The Seven Pillars of Positive Energy

What is a pillar?

A pillar is a fundamental *principle,* rule, and/or practice upon which something depends. It provides strength, *identity* and *substance.*

So, the seven pillars of positive energy are the various *sources* from which our energy needs can be met. Keep in mind that energy isn't just a physical entity. We also draw energy from our emotions, clarity of thought, as well as the meaningful and fulfilling events in our lives.

For instance, to feel alive, not only do we have to practice daily health-building habits, we must also clarify and *understand why we do the things we do* — both at work and in our personal lives, cultivate positive emotions, and make time for play.

From my experience researching and consulting with private clients, there are seven sources of positive energy that are the foundation of an energized life. They are as follows:

Pillar #1: Passion and Purpose

Ask yourself this question. When do you feel most energized? Is it when you're doing things that you don't really enjoy or find meaningful? Or is it when you're so fully engaged that you lose track of time and everything else that's going on around you?

Are you energized by the constant demand on your time? Does your work leave you drained or fulfilled at the end of the day?

It is not possible to fully energize your life if you spend most or all of your working hours in work that you don't find in alignment with your core values.

While it's a reality that millions of people spend their days at jobs that they hate, a more powerful scenario is to learn to love your work or make plans to move on ("love it or leave it"). You either reconnect with your "why," the purpose behind the work that you do, or create a plan to exit.

If your work doesn't fuel you with positive energy, you need to get reenergized by a) reminding yourself why you do the work, or by b) reconnecting with the purpose that your current job serves in your life at the moment.

However, sometimes in order to live with passion and purpose you have to be willing to cut the rope of security and learn how to get paid to do what you love.

You may find, as I did over twenty years ago, that what awaits you is freedom, fulfillment and fun.

Pillar #2: Personal Evolution

Expansion is the natural state of the universe. If you're not expanding or evolving, then you're dying.

To live an energized life you must be willing to *take risks* and reconnect with your *innate curiosity*. If you watch toddlers, they get into everything because they're curious. That's how they learn and grow.

Adults tend to forget that it's also how we *learn and grow.* It's how we *evolve.* It's how we help our brain *make new* connections, even as we get older.

Although evolution is a natural process that is taking place with or without our cooperation, we can tap into this enormous force of nature to make our lives better in many ways.

To align ourselves with the force of evolution, we have to *develop deeper self-awareness.* As Deepak Chopra said, "Awareness wants to expand and evolve; this natural tendency has always been part of your makeup."

Pillar #3: Physical Vitality

The human body is meant to move. The more it moves, the more energy it generates.

As you push your body beyond your comfort zone, you will reach a level of exuberant physical vigor. This will dramatically increase your physical energy capacity.

And since we experience our lives through the body, physical vitality is one of the most important of the seven pillars because it *directly affects our thoughts, emotions, energy level, and all the other pillars.*

Therefore, it is not possible to fully energize your life without first building a solid physical foundation.

Pillar #4: Positive Energy

Most people think of energy only in terms of their physical capacity, meaning, whether they are feeling energized or depleted. However, energy can be thought of in two ways. It can be thought of as either the capacity to do work, or as a life force that can heal or — when blocked — cause disease.

Like electricity, *energy has a charge.* It can either be *positive or negative.* Positive energy is light. It gives us focus, joy and meaning. Negative energy is heavy and dark. It depletes us, leads to bad judgment, loss of creativity and confusion.

Our positive energy capacity is limited and can be easily depleted. If not renewed regularly, we go into survival mode. In survival mode, our energy has a negative charge. Therefore we feel exhausted, fatigued, angry, resentful, unfulfilled, and lack focus.

While this is a natural part of the energy cycle, in order to energize your life, your objective should be to move through this negative energy phase as quickly as possible. To do this, however, requires a greater degree of energy awareness.

Pillar #5: Positive Psychology

Science is finally catching up with what most of us already knew: *our psychology controls our biology.*

For years, the science of psychology has been focused on what's wrong with people. However, the new field of *positive psychology* focuses on *what is right in our lives* and how we can finally use this scientific knowledge to lead better lives.

This new field of positive psychology has generated some important scientific discoveries. For instance, studies confirm that *the way we think about our setbacks* and negative life circumstances is the real cause of depression, the feeling of helplessness, and many stress-related disorders.

We also know that *positive emotions affect the brain's biochemistry and lead to positive outcomes.* Therefore, you can make your life better by cultivating positive emotions, and by changing your thought process when you experience negative setbacks.

Pillar #6: Prosocial Behavior

Did you know that *doing good is also good for you?* That's right. Performing unselfish acts of kindness is what social scientists call "prosocial behavior." And when you help others your behavior actually changes the biochemistry of your brain.

You feel warm and fuzzy inside because your good deeds trigger the brain to release certain neurochemicals that make you feel good.

A number of studies have also concluded that cancer patients, who go out of their way to help other cancer patients, recover faster and live longer.

It pays to be good after all.

Pillar #7: Play

Playfulness, laughter and fun stimulate creativity, rejuvenate your soul, and make you feel alive again.

Laughter not only makes you feel good, it also stimulates biochemical reactions in the body that have a positive effect on your immune system.

Play is a state of being. It is purposeless, fun and pleasurable. In play, the focus is entirely on the experience in the moment, instead of accomplishing a particular goal.

Play is a profound biological process. It shapes the brain, fosters empathy and is the doorway to our creative selves.

In play is when we feel most alive.

Ignite Your Passions…Fuel Your Purpose

"A man needs a little madness, or else…"
– Zorba the Greek

Pillar #1: Passion & Purpose

Passion energizes. Purpose motivates.

When we're passionately engaged in an activity, we experience a sense of freedom and inner calm. Our passions energize us and make us feel alive again.

Passion leads to full engagement, which often leads to a state that psychologist Mihaly Csikszentmihalyi calls "flow."

When in a state of "flow", we're so fully engaged in the activity that nothing else seems to matter. Csikszentmihalyi writes in his book, *Flow*, "the experience itself is so enjoyable that people will do it even at great cost, for the sheer sake of doing it."

So what is a passion?

A passion is a strong desire for — or devotion to — an activity or concept that is pursued for its own sake.

We pursue our passions even at great personal cost because *they make us feel alive*. They take us to a place beyond our daily worries and frustrations.

In our pursuits, we are *often stretched beyond our preconceived limits*. So, the very act of participating in our passions may be painful, but in the end, we are made better.

What is your passion? Everyone has one. Some of us have many.

In high school, I was fanatical about Chinese martial arts. I practiced day and night, in sunshine, rain or snow. My martial arts practice led to a passion for philosophy, fitness and dance.

I pursued these activities even at great personal expense, but, my practice led to a feeling of mastery and self-control. So, in 1994 when I said goodbye to corporate America, I chose to pursue my passions — teaching fitness, dance, and martial arts.

Over the years I have added new passions such as tennis, skiing, and sharing ideas with others through writing and speaking. Interestingly, one passion often leads to another.

Remember, a passion is often pursued for its own sake. Sometimes it ends up being a good money-making venture and sometimes not.

In fact, when I decided to walk away from corporate America, my family and friends thought that I was mad. How could I walk away from a prestigious job with great benefits for the uncertainty of being on my own, doing what I loved to do?

Was it madness? Perhaps.

But sometimes in order to truly live, you have to be willing to try a little madness. As their entrepreneurial venture teeters on the verge of failure before it even gets started, Zorba councils Basil in the movie Zorba the Greek:

> *"A man needs a little madness, or else, he never dares cut the rope [of security] and be free."*

Remember, passion energizes and purpose motivates.

So what is your passion? Are you pursuing it?

It's also okay if you don't know what you're passionate about. Maybe you fell into a job or career that was a great opportunity at the time, became successful at it, and years later you're still doing the same thing even though it doesn't fulfill you.

The best way to find your passion is to try new things. Experience really is the best teacher.

For example, for years I thought tennis, golf and salsa music were boring and uninteresting. Yet today, nothing energizes me like a challenging game of tennis, hitting balls at the driving range, or losing myself on the dance floor to some old Afro-Cuban mambo music.

I've even traveled around the world performing and teaching Latin dance.

So, get out there and boldly *try something new*. Start with the things that you currently spend your time doing just for the love of it. Is there a way to teach others what you know?

Have you achieved a level of proficiency in something you've been doing as a hobby? Can you teach others?

Many years ago when I started practicing martial arts and salsa dancing, they were just hobbies. I had no intention of teaching. However, with years of practice came a level of proficiency that others also seek. Best of all, they are willing to pay me to teach them.

So, when you're searching for your passions, *always start with the things that you do for fun* then explore other areas.

Passion leads to purpose

It's pointless asking yourself what is the purpose of your life if you're sitting in some dead-end job. You have to get out into the world and test reality. You have to experience life through the pursuit of your passions in order to arrive at what feels most meaningful and fulfilling to you.

Instead of asking "what is my purpose?"…a better way of phrasing the question is "how am I allowing life to find its fullest expression through me?" Another good question to ask is "what is my big vision for my life?"

These are queries that can only be actualized through a life of passion and meaning. Anything less and you end up being a fragment of yourself, living a life of boredom and regret.

And as you already know, *boredom won't energize you, neither will regret.* You have to regularly engage in activities that make you feel alive.

You must also *find meaning in your work or create a plan to move on.* Going to a job everyday that doesn't inspire you does more than drain your vital life energy; it robs you of your humanity because, as surely as a bird instinctively knows how to fly, you were meant to aspire for greatness. *Greatness is in your DNA.*

You must claim your magnificence, proclaim your freedom, and start living your passions. This is how you give your life meaning. It is the only path that leads to a truly energized life.

Your Life's Purpose

We exist on this earth for a very short time and the purpose of our lives is "to live." I don't mean to simply exist.

Getting up in the morning and going to a job you hate, then coming home and watching television until you fall asleep, only to get up and repeat, isn't living; that's existing.

"To live" is a verb. This means that you have to take some conscious action in order to have an experience of life.

But, how do we experience life?

Well, *we experience life through our senses: smell, touch, taste, sight and sound.* Of course, we may also experience life on a deeper metaphysical level, but that's a topic for another day.

Therefore, to experience life, we have to get up off our butts and go smell the flowers, taste some good food, do something we don't know how to do, marvel at the beauty around us, and learn how to listen to the stillness of motion.

Our lives are nothing more than the accumulation of our experiences. Some will be memorable and others won't.

Those memorable experiences are what give our lives meaning. They bring us happiness and joy. They touch the lives of others and in doing so, make a difference in the world.

Those experiences that are less memorable serve simply as a way to kill time.

So, a better question to ask than "What is my life's purpose?" is *"What can I do with my time today that is meaningful — in some way — to me or others?"*

That could mean doing a small part to help solve one of the many problems of the world or it could mean just being a good friend.

Don't forget that *who you're being, is often more important than what you do.*

So, the purpose of your life is to live. To live vibrantly, love passionately, and make a difference in some way.

But here's the thing: When you're truly living life, you spend your time doing things that are important to you, and/or things that make a difference in other people's lives.

Important things tend to be meaningful and fulfilling and therefore, the purpose of your life is simply *to do things that are meaningful and fulfilling.*

And the truth is, it really doesn't matter what those things are, as long as they are meaningful and fulfilling to you.

Here's another secret, the things that we find most meaningful and fulfilling, the things that makes us feel most alive, are usually those things that we are most passionate about.

So, isn't it interesting that what gives our lives meaning and make us feel fulfilled and living on purpose is simply to be in pursuit of our passions.

However, *those passions must meet certain criteria.*

First, they must cause some degree of personal expansion. That is, you must be growing or evolving in some meaningful way because that is the natural order of life itself, to evolve or become more than what it is.

Second, our passions must in some way *make other people's lives better.* This is important because as we become less self-centered, we're able to open up to a bigger purpose of helping others lessen their suffering and experience more joy and happiness from life.

Therefore, to live on purpose is to experience the joy and happiness of being fully alive and to help others do the same.

So, when do we feel most alive? When we're in pursuit of our passions.

The Passion Manifesto:
Uncovering your passions

Everybody has a passion. Most of us have several.

I developed a passion for speaking in front of an audience when I was about seven or eight years old as an altar boy in the Catholic Church. I was always called upon to read bible passages or to speak on special occasions.

Today, I feel most alive when I'm either speaking or performing in front of an audience.

As a boy, I also loved to read philosophy and the works of great writers. Secretly, I developed an inner yearning to be able to express myself in writing as they did and to become a published author. This is my ninth book.

In high school, I was also crazy about Chinese martial arts. I went to classes six days a week, read every book I could get my hands on, watched every Chinese martial arts movie I could find, and participated in every tournament I could afford to attend. Thirty years later, practicing martial arts is still one of my many passions.

In fact, it was because of my martial arts training that I also developed a passion for personal growth, fitness and nutrition. Then came Latin dance, skate-dancing, tennis, skiing and trail running.

As you can see, I have many passions and so do you, though you may not remember what they are.

So, to live an exciting and meaningful life, your job is to first uncover your passions, or at least one, and learn to lose your mind and come to your senses.

If you're stuck and can't remember what you're passionate about, here are a few simple ideas to help you get unstuck, or simply to help you uncover the passions you never realized you had.

The Passion Manifesto:
Seven Keys to Uncovering Your Passions

1. Embarrass yourself often

Let's face it; most of us don't like to embarrass ourselves. We also don't like to look foolish.

Unfortunately, before you can be great at something, anything, you have to first suck at it and in order to get better at it, you have to embarrass yourself in some way, either in class or with a coach or instructor.

This is the main reason why most of us shy away from doing new things, because who likes to look foolish doing something they're not good at? But the problem is, *if you avoid doing things that are embarrassing, you will never end up doing anything truly important,* because you'll be too afraid to try new things.

So, embrace embarrassment. Sometimes looking foolish is a part of the growth process necessary to accomplish meaningful things.

2. Lose yourself in something

In my youth, I used to practice martial arts for several hours at a time. Often I would show up an hour before class and stay an hour after class. It wasn't that I loved to feel pain, I just loved getting better and the better I got, the harder I practiced, because I loved the feeling of being able to do things that I couldn't do before.

Today, that same passion for personal growth serves me well as an entrepreneur because I often need to learn new things and I love the challenge of figuring things out.

I'm sure that you too have had the experience of getting so lost in some activity that minutes turned into hours and before you knew it, you'd forgotten to eat or go to sleep.

The activity is so important. It doesn't matter whether it's reading a good novel, painting or trying to solve a problem. The act of losing yourself in some activity will reveal one of your true passions. It may not be the activity itself, but it may very well be the reason why you do the activity in the first place.

So find something that enthralls you and lose yourself in it. Passion awaits you.

3. Tackle a BIG problem that matters to the world

The truth is, the world doesn't need saving. It existed long before humans were part of the equation and it will continue to exist long after we're here.

However, there are quite a few problems facing the world today whose solutions could make life a lot better for all of us.

Certainly you're not going to solve the world's problems, but you can do your small part in making a difference.

Whether it's world hunger, climate change, human trafficking, obesity — any issue that speaks to you — you can make a difference in someone's life.

And when we make a difference in other people's lives, it gives meaning and fulfillment to our own.

So, do as Gandhi recommended and *"be now the change you wish to see in the world."* You may just uncover your passion for helping others.

4. Be very good at something

It's very difficult to be passionate about something when you have no experience with anything. People who are passionate about computer programming spend a lot of time learning everything they can about programming.

Since high school, I have read every book, watched every movie, and attended as many martial arts tournaments and symposiums as I could. Why? To expand my knowledge.

When you're passionate about something, that's what you do; you get good at it. And if you stick with it long enough, your passion leads to mastery.

Here's a little secret for you: when you've attained mastery at anything it carries over into other areas because *mastery is first and foremost a mindset*. It's a way of approaching the things that you do.

5. Revisit what you enjoyed doing at age 10

Sometimes, the things that we were most passionate about when we were kids still have special meaning to us. Unfortunately, when we were young, most of us were encouraged to move away from the things that brought us the most joy to other areas that seemed more practical.

So what did you really enjoy doing as a young boy or girl? Revisit that time in your life and you may discover your pot of gold.

6. Use trial and error

As I've said before, it's hard to be passionate about something when you have very little experience doing anything. So, take some time to go out and try new things. If you don't know what line of work to get into, go volunteer somewhere, become a clerk, get an internship, just try something.

Just reading about something won't tell you very much. You have to get out there and have an experience. We learn through our experiences. Just reading about something won't tell you if you're going to find it fulfilling; you have to experience it.

7. Imagine a world without you

Some people are paralyzed by the realization that their lives thus far have been unfulfilled. They've spent their lives chasing after success yet they still feel unfulfilled and without a purpose.

In fact, I have coached very successful clients in their fifties who felt lost and without purpose.

The problem is that in all our busyness, we lose sight of what life is really about. *The purpose of life is "to live." It is to find things that we are passionate about and do them regularly.* As well as to make a difference in the lives of others.

The things that we are passionate about are usually those we find meaningful and important. One way that I like to think about what's important to me is to think about what personal legacy I'm leaving behind.

So, *imagine sitting on your deathbed, reflecting on your life.* Did you *live fully?* Did you *make a difference?* Did your life matter at all or did you live a life of insignificance?

What personal legacy are you leaving behind? What did you do that was significant to the world?

Did your life find its fullest expression through you?

Find an answer to these questions and you most definitely will live a life of passion and purpose.

Love It or Leave It: Creating Fulfilling Work

*"People are always blaming their circumstances for what they are.
I don't believe in circumstances.
The people who get on in this world are the people who get up
and look for the circumstances they want, and,
if they can't find them, make them."*
– George Bernard Shaw

Let's be clear about something, it's not always possible to follow your passion in the workplace. The old saying, "Do what you love and the money will follow," is not always true.

Likewise, if you're just starting your career, sometimes the advice to follow your passion may lead you down a never-ending path of constantly switching jobs. Why does this happen? It happens because you're in search of something that is quite elusive in most workplace — passion.

Often, passion in the workplace comes after spending years honing your skills and attaining a level of mastery.

This fact, however, should not be an excuse to remain stuck in work that is neither fulfilling nor growth enhancing.

Your work should serve a purpose. Maybe for you, it's a way to cover your daily expenses while you pursue your true passion on the side. For others, it may be a way to get the necessary experience they need.

For many employees, especially those who are just getting started in the "real world," they just work for a paycheck in order to pay their monthly expenses until they figure out what they really want to do with their lives.

Whatever your reason for working, you have to ask yourself, *do you really enjoy what you do? Do you love it? Did you once love what you do for work, but now "the thrill is gone?"*

It's time to be honest with yourself. If you work at a job or even as a self-employed person, you most likely spend more time at work than anywhere else.

So, do you really want to continue to endure what Dostoyevsky called the most terrible human punishment: to be condemned to a lifetime of work that is "completely and utterly devoid of usefulness and meaning?"

To work with meaning is to work with purpose. Without purpose, there can be no passion. Without passion, your work will just become another "energy sucker," slowing sucking the life out of you until there's nothing left but bitterness and regret.

The good news: *if you're not in love with your work,* you can either learn to love it or create a plan to leave it. But first you have to start with 'why?' Why do you do the work that you currently do? This is not about self-judgment, however, there is power in knowing why you get up in the mornings and spend so much of your time each day at work.

What drives you? Are you driven by "extrinsic" or "intrinsic" motivating factors?

In his book, *How to Find Fulfilling Work*, Roman Krznaric wrote that "earning money, achieving status, making a difference, following our passions, and using our talents…are the five fundamental motivating forces that drive people in their careers."

If you *work primarily to pursue money and status*, these would be considered 'extrinsic' motivating factors since you're approaching work as a *means to an end*.

The other three are 'intrinsic' motivating factors since work is valued as an end in itself.

Knowing what motivates you and knowing why you're doing the work that you're currently doing is the key to developing what Krznaric calls a "personal vision of what meaningful work looks like."

What motivates YOU?

Learning to Love Your Work

If you're motivated by intrinsic factors, yet you're working primarily for money or status, you don't have to leave your job to find meaning.

You can use your job to support yourself while you pursue your true passions. Of course, you may have to reorganize your schedule to give yourself more time to pursue other endeavors.

In this way, you're never really stuck doing work that you don't love. You're simply using your job to finance your true passion.

Can you use your non-working hours to hone your skills or develop a greater degree of mastery around your passions?

Can you develop a business around your passions so that you can ultimately turn your passion into profit? The possibilities are endless.

Do you see how changing your view of work can instantly energize you? Instead of looking at your work as something you do to pass the time, you can now see your employer as the financer of your bigger vision.

The venture capitalist investing in "YOU, Incorporated."

On the other hand, if you once loved your work, but lost your passion for it, you may need to rediscover what you loved about it in the first place.

Did you love the technical or creative aspect of your work but now find yourself pushing paper or feeling lost in the operational or managerial side of your business?

What was it that you loved about your work and if doing that is really what gives you a sense of meaning and purpose, how can you get it back?

When you reconnect with your 'why' or the purpose that your work serves in your life, it can fill you with positive energy and bring new life to your work.

It doesn't matter if your work only serves as a paycheck while you pursue your true passions on the side. The important thing is to always work with a sense of purpose and know why you're doing what you're doing.

Remember: passion energizes and purpose motivates.

Now, I realize that doing a bunch of mental gymnastics probably won't get you to love a job that you truly hate or find boring, so I'll leave out the mind tricks that most career success experts usually recommend.

However, keep in mind that time is a precious resource that you can never get back. So, even if you hate your job, I would encourage you to always *think like a business owner.*

Is there *something you do at work that you could get better at?* Can you develop a marketable skill around some of the tasks that you do daily?

What can you learn in your current job today that can help you to be a successful entrepreneur in the next two to three years?

Or, if entrepreneurship isn't your cup of tea, what is your ideal job?

If you were to do as Krznaric recommends and write a personal job advertisement — listing your passions, qualities, values, and skills — what would your "WANTED" ad look like?

If you're unhappy at work, don't just 'grin and bear it' or complain about your job, be proactive and do something about it.

First, *write an ad for your ideal job* as I mentioned above. What skills, talents, qualities, and values have you identified as necessary for your new job?

Next, take the time now to start *developing the skills and talents you're going to need* and start embodying the qualities and values of the person you'll need to become for your ideal job.

In short, *start becoming the person you need to become to attract your new job*. Quite frankly, I can't imagine anyone being successful at any job if they sit around all day bored and complaining.

So, be proactive and never complain about your job because you have CHOSEN to be where you are. You are free to leave or change careers whenever you choose.

My wife is a great example of someone who decided, "enough is enough" and switched careers from marketing to nursing.

While in the hospital after the birth of our first daughter, she had an epiphany that nursing would be a great career choice for her, and would fulfill her longing to do something that makes a difference in people's lives.

She gave birth in November and by February she was back in school taking her nursing prerequisites. She even brought the baby and a nanny on campus with her so she could breastfeed between classes.

Well, four years and three kids later (we had twins a year-and-a-half after our first daughter was born), my wife is now a registered nurse. Was it easy? Definitely not. It was scary. She doubted herself and her decision and there were times when she wanted to quit.

But the important thing is she persevered. She graduated nursing school, passed her state board exam, and is now working in a hospital making a difference in people's lives.

How do I know she's making a difference? Her patients tell her so.

Don't waste your life sitting at a job you hate, working with people you would never want to hang out with. You and only you are responsible for your own happiness.

If my wife can get through nursing school while taking care of three toddlers, what's stopping you?

Remember, going everyday to a job that you hate is a major "energy sucker" and so is complaining about it. But, lacking the courage to move away from such situations is an even a bigger energy drain.

When we develop the courage to get in the ring and spar with our fears and say to them "go away and don't ever come back," as Gollum did in the movie *Lord of the Rings: Return of the King*, only then will we also find the courage to say "enough of this! I'm not going to put up with this anymore!"

What awaits you on the other side is what motivates us most – a feeling of autonomy, mastery, and connection with your peers.

I hope you can join us there.

Before You Ditch Your Day Job:
Not Everyone is Cutout to Be an Entrepreneur.

Entrepreneurs are creators.

We are people who value above all else the freedom to create our own fate. We value personal fulfillment and the opportunity to pursue our passions above the "security" of a regular paycheck.

Entrepreneurs live with uncertainty. Not knowing where the next client is coming from, or whether your business idea will succeed or fail.

To those of us who made the leap of faith, as I did over twenty years ago, this kind of freedom and uncertainty is exhilarating.

To others who haven't yet shed their conditioning to go to college, study in a marketable field, then get a good job with benefits, the prospect of starting from nothing and creating a business based on their passions might be terrifying.

So it's up to you to decide if you have what it takes to choose freedom over security.

Explorer Chris McCandless said it best in the book (about him), *Into the Wild:*

> *"So many people live with unhappy circumstances and yet will not take the initiative to change their situation because they are conditioned to a life of security, conformity, and conservatism, all of which may appear to give one peace of mind, but in reality nothing is more damaging to the adventurous spirit within a [person] than a secure future."*

Ultimately, *if freedom, fulfillment and the pursuit of your passion are what you're after, it's going to take a little madness* or you won't dare to cut the rope of security and be free.

How do you know when is the right time to get started? You won't. *The right time is now, so go ahead and get started.*

By this, I don't mean irresponsibly quitting your day job without a plan in place to support yourself and your family.

First, you have to clarify what your passions are and what new business venture you can develop based on one or more of your passions. You also have to think about how you're going to fund your new venture until you start making some sales.

Yes, I did say sales. You're going to have to sell something to make money.

So, what I mean by 'get started now' is that the best time to start *formulating your plan is now*. Come up with a plan and start your business on the side while you still have a job.

Use the skills that you've developed from working to start your business part-time and get it to where it's making money.

Before I left my job in corporate America I was already teaching martial arts and fitness on the side. So, all I had to do before I walked out the door was to figure out how to scale my business to replace my income.

If you don't have a clue how to get started and go about turning your passion into a viable business venture, check out my good friend and college buddy Walt Goodridge's book, *Turn Your Passion Into Profit*.

I like Walt's philosophy. He writes that everyone has a passion, every passion has value, and any passion can be turned into profit. Therefore, freedom is achievable.

In his book, he also takes you through quite a few discovery exercises to help you uncover your passions, come up with your passion ideas or business concepts, and develop a plan to turn those ideas into a viable product or service.

Don't worry if you discover that you have many passions. As a matter of fact, I hope you do, because as an entrepreneur you're going to have to develop multiple sources of income in order to insulate yourself from the uncertainty of the marketplace.

To be successful, you're going to have to become what Krznaric calls a "wide achiever." Instead of aspiring to be a high achiever in one narrow field of specialization, you might be more fulfilled by developing multiple talents and interests.

Krznaric writes:

"There are two classic approaches to being a wide achiever: becoming a 'Renaissance generalist', who pursues several careers simultaneously, or a 'serial specialist', who does one after another."

In my case, I've chosen to express my various passions as a 'Renaissance generalist'. I've been able to make a living as a Nutritionist, fitness instructor, author, columnist, martial arts instructor, dance instructor, professional speaker, coach and consultant.

These are all intrinsically rewarding activities that utilize my talents, express my passions, and make a difference in the world.

Finally, keep in mind that the most successful entrepreneurs are those who have found ways to turn their passions into multiple streams of income. So it's never too early to start thinking about how to develop a business around your passions.

Another great option is a part-time home-based business as an independent distributor for a product or company whose mission is in alignment with your own. This is a great way to develop the necessary business and entrepreneurial skills you will need to turn your passions into profit, and to live a life of freedom, fulfillment, and fun.

Are you ready to become a creator? Why not start today?

Start with WHY

As you embark upon the rest of your life, whether as an employee or as an entrepreneur, I hope you remember one thing, always start with 'WHY'.

Ask yourself often, why am I here? Why did I CHOOSE to take this job? Why have I chosen to stay? Why would I be better served if I choose to make a change?

The answers to these questions will empower and inspire you. You will either discover renewed energy in your work or the confidence to start developing your exit strategy.

If you discover a little madness in you and choose to pursue the path of the entrepreneur, remember that your primary job is to be a leader.

To be a leader you must have followers. But, you can't make people follow you. You must inspire them to want to follow you because they share your vision.

Where does vision come from? It comes from having a clearly defined purpose or a clearly defined WHY.

As Simon Sinek wrote in his book, *Start with Why:*

> *"Our visions are the world we imagine, the tangible results of what the world would look like if we spend every day in pursuit of our WHY."*

When we live and work with passion and purpose, we will energize our lives and make a significant difference in the world because every day is spent in pursuit of our WHY.

Passion-Purpose Action Plan

Step 1: Create Your Ideal Scene

- If you could **change anything** in your life what would it be? **Why?**
- If all your monthly expenses were covered, what would you **spend your time doing everyday?**

Step 2: Ignite Your Passions

- What do you like to do **that gives you the most joy** (your "joy activity")?
- What would you **have to give up** in order to incorporate your joy activity (s) in your life at least twice per week?
- If you could spend your time "working" to **master one activity,** what would that activity be? Are you proficient enough to **teach it right now?**

Step 3: Fuel Your Life with Purpose

- What can you do with your time today that is **meaningful to you or others?**
- In what small way can you **make a difference** in someone else's life today?
- If the definition of LIFE is: Living In Full Expression, how could you **inject more LIFE into your day** (at work, at home and at play)?

Step 4: Find or Create Fulfilling Work

- Why do you **do the work you currently do?**
- Is your work **engaging, fulfilling,** and does it **stimulate growth?**
- Is your work **meaningful to you** or would you **rather pursue something else?** What (different assignment, different depart ment, or a different career path)?
- If you're unhappy with your work, **what would you change,** if you could? If you can't change anything, what's your **exit strategy?**
- What is your **ideal work scenario** and how can you start **creating it today? What skills will you need** to master to be successful and can you start developing them now?
- If freedom, fulfillment and fun are what you seek, can you start developing a **part-time business** around one or more of your passions?
- Is there a **home-based business opportunity,** whose mission is in alignment with your own, that you could pursue to start making an income now?

Get Exclusive Extras at *EnergizedLifeAcademy.com*

~ Energize Your Life Action Plan workbook

**~ 7 Questions (to Ask Yourself) to Help You
Fuel Your Life with Purpose, Passion & Play ebook**

~ Free coaching videos on all seven pillars

Energize Your Life

3

Accelerate Your Personal Evolution

*"Every talent we cultivate brings to mind
the desire to cultivate another talent;
we are subject to the urge of life, seeking
expression, which ever drives us on to know
more, to do more, and to be more."*

Pillar #2: Personal Evolution

We are the vehicles through which life finds its full expression.

We are born with an innate curiosity to learn new things, to ignore all boundaries, and to grow.

A seed planted in fertile soil has the mission to reach for the sun and when it can no longer get there, it produces more seeds to continue the process of life. We humans live by the same urge to seek fuller expression. *Personal evolution is our natural tendency.*

But, this physical process of personal growth is also accompanied by an *innate curiosity to explore both our inner and outer worlds.*

Just watch a toddler as she explores the world around her through her senses. She possesses a natural curiosity to want to know what things are and *why*.

As she further develops her awareness, every answer she gets to her questions will be accompanied by another question—'why?'

Why is that, daddy? Why is the sky blue? Why is the grass green?

This is nature's way of helping her expand her awareness of self and the world around.

In fact, we were all born with this inherent tendency to expand awareness and as our inner awareness expands, we become more conscious of our *unresolved issues*.

As we get to know ourselves better, our lives will also get better because we become less reactive to the stressors around us.

We develop the ability to a*nalyze our inner and outer environments, make emotionally free judgments* about our situations, draw *clear, informed conclusions,* and form *thoughtful plans of action.*

In short, we become more adaptable to our changing environment, and thus, able to respond to our circumstances without the negative emotional energy.

So, it's not that the world will suddenly change, it's more that your improved ability to function in the world will allow you to deal with 'problems' before they become crises.

I'm sure you've noticed that when you are in *crisis mode* it *automatically triggers your fight-or-flight survival instinct,* which usually leads to a *negative emotional response.*

Well, this negative emotional response is what sucks your energy. And unfortunately, most of us experience this several times a day.

To truly energize your life, you have to choose to participate in your personal evolution.

As a child, this process of evolutionary growth happened naturally. However, as adults, our focus shifts from expanding self-awareness, to earning a living and supporting our families.

As you make the choice to participate in your own conscious evolution, however, you will develop new self-awareness skills that help you to be less reactive to your daily stressors.

And as you become less reactive and more responsive to your environment, you improve your ability to get rid of many of the 'energy suckers' in your life. This increases your positive energy.

So, the first step on the path to personal evolution is to consciously seek to expand your awareness — to understand your own character, habits, thoughts, feelings, desires and emotions.

Self-awareness is the **key** that opens the door to **personal evolution**.

As you become aware of your habits, thoughts and emotions, you are able to change the unconscious scripts in your brain that control your bad habits and energy-draining behaviors.

In short, self-awareness helps you to rewire the brain for good habits. And good habits increase your positive energy, which energizes your life.

"The aim of life is to live,
and to live means to be aware,
joyously, drunkenly, serenely,
divinely aware." – Henry Miller

7 Ways to Expand Your Self-Awareness

*"We don't see things as they are,
we see them as we are."*
– Anais Nin

1. Become a "Neutral Observer"

One of the best ways to expand your self-awareness and learn who you really are is to observe yourself in action.

To do this, you have to imagine that there are many aspects to your SELF. *The SELF is your whole being* and the SELF has multiple personalities that are a result of your unresolved issues and irrational beliefs.

One such aspect of personality could be the 'wounded inner child'. Another might be the 'narcissist'. These are all different for each of us. They're not good or bad; they're just personality traits based on where we are in our own personal evolution.

So, it isn't far-fetched to think that you can just sit back as a 'neutral observer' and watch all these different personality aspects interact with the world.

The key here is to observe without judgment. Just practice watching yourself as if you were a separate person watching someone else, except, the person you're watching is yourself.

This may sound a bit off-the-wall but it really is a very simple and powerful practice that can teach you more about yourself than anything else you might do.

Again, the key is to practice being both 'the observer' and 'the observed' in your daily life. As you practice this, you will start asking yourself some very important self-reflecting questions such as "why did I do that?" or "why did that make me feel this way?"

This is important because self-awareness, or *knowing yourself, is the essence of personal evolution.* And the more you know yourself, the less reactive you will be to outside stimuli. The less reactive you are, the more you will remain a conduit for positive energy.

Positive energy is energizing. Negative energy is draining. To energize your life you must remain a conduit for positive energy.

2. See with NEW Eyes

One of the nice benefits of thirty plus years of martial arts practice is that I am intimately aware of everyone and everything around me. The first thing I do when I come into any new environment is to slowly "check it out." By that I mean that I observe everything that is happening within the first thirty seconds of being there. I like to observe the various actors and the different scenes that are playing out right in front of me.

I try to really "see" what's happening — as if what I'm looking at contains the answers to the deep mysteries of life.

Most people don't see what's around them. Unfortunately, they only casually glance at the mysteries of life unfolding in front of their very eyes. They couldn't tell you what color clothes the person who just walked right by was wearing. They're too preoccupied, lost in their own world, and unaware of the beauty of life progressing around them.

Expanding awareness requires that we begin to see the world with 'new eyes' – with eyes that really see what's happening.

Look at those beautiful flowers you just walked by. Oh, was that a bed of white roses? Did you take a moment to smell them?

Look at the two squirrels chasing each other up and down the tree, did you notice? Did you notice the smile on the face of the person who just walked right by you in the crosswalk?

This is what it means to see the world with new eyes. It means to really observe the little things, because that is where the mystery unfolds.

When we are aware of what is happening around us, it helps us to *better understand and appreciate our connection with the rest of the world.*

3. "Check-in" regularly

What are you thinking this very moment? What are you feeling?

The first level of self-awareness requires that we become aware of our emotions in specific situations. How does it make me feel when I have to deal with abrasive people? How do I feel when someone gives me feedback on my behavior?

Developing emotional self-awareness is an important step on the path to personal evolution. However, our emotions are preceded by a thought process, so in order to change how we feel, we have to also be aware of what we're thinking.

The simplest way of becoming aware of what we're thinking and feeling is to develop a habit of 'checking-in' on a regular basis. Whenever you feel upset or irritated by someone or something, pause for just a moment and ask yourself a few questions:

- What am I thinking right now'?
- What am I feeling right now?
- What irrational beliefs am I holding onto that cause me to feel this way?

We hold irrational beliefs in our heads about how things "should" be. This belief system becomes the driving force behind how we think, feel and act in most situations.

Know this: *the very act of pausing to 'check-in' will ultimately help to expand your emotional self-awareness and contribute to your personal evolution.*

4. Identify your negative emotional triggers

An emotional trigger is an experience that takes you back to the past, stirring up old feelings and behaviors. So obviously, *negative emotional triggers will bring up past negative experiences.*

For instance, a domineering boss may remind you of your bad relationship with your dad, or your gossiping coworkers may trigger feelings of old high school or college cliques.

It doesn't matter what the specific situation is, the important thing is to be able to identity the triggers that cause your brain to take you through your old behavioral patterns that no longer serve you.

The key is to catch yourself reacting when you are triggered. Obviously, this is going to take some practice to develop the ability to be aware of your emotional state in the midst of an emotional storm.

However, we are often triggered when our brain perceives that we are not getting or will not be getting something that we highly value. Such as: acceptance, autonomy, safety, being understood, being valued, feeling respected, feeling heard, being in control, etc.

As before, practice 'checking-in' during these emotional storms, and ask yourself this question: Which of my needs are not being met at this moment?

The better you become at identifying your unmet needs the more control you will have over your emotional state. By being aware of which unmet needs are serving as negative emotional triggers, over time this awareness will free you to respond differently.

Self-awareness leads to emotional maturity.
Without emotional maturity, negative emotional triggers enslave us.

5. Practice "thought watching"

"Thought watching" is a popular practice in meditation. The idea is to sit quietly and practice watching your thoughts as they flash across the 'screen' of your mind, like the scenes of a movie on a movie screen.

Only, instead of sitting quietly and trying to watch my thoughts without getting too engaged with any one of them, I prefer to practice 'thought watching' while engaging in my normal daily life.

If the idea is to become aware of what I'm thinking, which it is, then I want to be aware of what I'm thinking while I'm engaging in daily interactions with people.

There is value in thought awareness because, as I mentioned before, our *thoughts dictate our feelings*. Our feelings control our actions.

So, just like checking-in, or identifying emotional triggers, "thought watching" is also best done while interacting with others.

All you have to do is get in the habit of regularly invoking your 'neutral observer' self and just follow your thoughts for a minute or two. Don't 'try' to do anything; just go where they go.

If one thought takes you deep into the minutia of your limiting beliefs, go with it and observe how your mind works. The idea is to see where you go and how you get there so that you will ultimately realize that you have the power to take control of your own mind.

As usual, the only objective of this exercise is to observe without judgment. This will allow you to develop a deeper awareness of your mind in action.

6. Learn to Manage Your Internal Dialogue

Do you talk to yourself? Whether you are aware of it or not, you do. In fact, everybody does.

The question is, when you talk to yourself are you invoking your *'inner-critic' or your 'inner-counselor'*? In our self-talk, most of us tend to be very critical and judgmental.

There are many reasons why one's 'inner-critic' is often louder than the 'inner-counselor'. Most of us had parents, teachers and coaches who were all very critical of our behaviors and abilities. In turn, we internalized those practices of being critical and judgmental in our conversations with self and others.

So as you can see, we've had a lot more practice invoking our inner-critics than we do listening to our inner-counselors.

But, have you noticed that negative inner dialogue leads to negative results, while positive inner dialogue most often leads to positive results?

I have tested this theorem on many occasions, especially during my weekly tennis games.

When you play an individual sport it is very easy to observe your internal dialogue because your inner-critic or inner-counselor shows up automatically after every single point.

In the past, if I won a point I would give myself positive feedback and if I lost the point I would berate myself. I would say things like "God you're so stupid!" Or "I'm such an idiot, how could I have missed that shot!"

Often after berating myself for missing a shot, I would start thinking that I'm going to miss the next shot, which often becomes a self-fulfilling prophecy.

Fortunately, because I regularly practice the earlier mentioned awareness techniques (neutral observer, check-in, thought watching, etc.), even in the middle of a tennis game, I am now able to silence my inner-critic and invoke my inner-counselor whether I win or lose a point.

This makes it a lot more enjoyable to play tennis because I no longer think about winning or losing. My primary objective is to play an 'inspired' game.

So how can you learn to silence your inner-critic and invoke your inner-counselor? You first have to become aware of the conversations that you're having with yourself.

This will happen during your daily practice; being a neutral observer, checking in or thought watching.

If you catch yourself judging, analyzing and being critical of yourself and others, change the conversation. Get in the habit of being encouraging, instead of critical.

Change the words that you use. Change what you're thinking about to *something more meaningful*.

And when it comes to others, realize that your inner counselor is wise and compassionate, not critical and judgmental.

So, practice invoking your inner-counselor more often and learn to silence your inner-critic.

7. Spend Time Alone

"I'll speak to thee in silence" — Shakespeare

Spending time alone is your chance to reflect, get re-acquainted with yourself, and to find your own voice. It is also a great time to practice some of the above mentioned self-awareness techniques.

By spending time alone, I don't mean on the phone, online, playing games or watching television. What I mean is spending time alone in silence, where you can sit with your thoughts and reflect on your life.

You don't have to be in solitude, in order to do this. One of my favorite ways to spend time alone whenever I visit New York City is to walk around the city — especially Central Park — and people watch.

When I'm back home in Los Angeles, I like to walk on the beach, watch the waves, or go for a hike in the Santa Monica Mountains.

When you spend time alone, it increases your *awareness of what you're thinking and feeling*. It also sharpens your intuition because you don't have to be talking all the time. You can simply just observe life as it unfolds.

It's important to make time to be in solitude, if not every day, at least once per week. Solitude expands your self-awareness and it also enhances the quality of your relationship with yourself and others.

If you have a very busy daily schedule, it's important to force yourself to disconnect from the rest of the world for even just a few minutes. If you have an office, close the door and put up a sign that you'll be back in five minutes.

Have lunch by yourself away from your desk and preferably away from your office at least once per week and don't spend that time running errands. Instead, take a walk or just sit in the park watching the squirrels chase each other up and down the trees.

What better way to enhance your self-awareness than to sit or take a walk in silence and simply observe life as it unfolds before your very eyes?

Personal Evolution Action Plan

Over the next week, practice the following awareness skills during your interactions with others, especially those who often push your buttons.

Step 1: **Practice being a Neutral Observer**

- To do this, imagine that there is a part of you that is separate from the one having the conversation. That's your Neutral Observer self who just observes without judgment. Focus on what you're thinking and feeling in the moment.

Step 2: **Identify your irrational beliefs**

The next time you're upset over your interaction with someone or some event, ask yourself three questions:

- **What am I thinking right now?**
- **What am I feeling right now?**
- **What beliefs am I holding onto** about how things "should" be (irrational beliefs) that is causing me to feel upset?

Step 3: **Practice identifying your negative emotional triggers**

- When an event or interaction with someone leads to a negative emotional reaction, ask yourself, which of my needs are not being met (acceptance, understanding, value, respect, autonomy, control, safety, etc.)?

Step 4: **Practice invoking your inner-counselor and silencing your inner-critic**

- When things don't go as you expect them to, **practice being encouraging and positive toward yourself and others**, instead of critical and judgmental.

Get Exclusive Extras at *EnergizedLifeAcademy.com*

~ **Energize Your Life Action Plan workbook**

~ **7 Questions (to Ask Yourself) to Help You
Fuel Your Life with Purpose, Passion & Play ebook**

~ **Free coaching videos on all seven pillars**

Energize Your Life

Cultivate Physical Vitality

"There is a vitality, a life force, an energy, a quickening,
that is translated through you into action,
and because there is only one of you in all time,
this expression is unique."
– Martha Graham

Pillar #3: Physical Vitality

Energy is both the capacity to do work and the life force that drives us toward meaning and purpose.

Vitality is a measure of our life force.

People with vitality often seem to have that special "something," yet you just can't put your finger on exactly what it is. Not only do they seem to radiate inner calm, they also have the energy to get more done. They attract others to them because they're fully present and more engaging.

Physical vitality is a state of complete physical, mental and social wellbeing, coupled with a high degree of life force energy.

People who possess physical vitality are usually happy, energetic, and very social. They radiate good health with sparkling eyes, healthy hair and skin, and are often the poster children for successful aging.

Why should physical vitality be important to you?

Over the years I've often shared with my clients that health isn't just about the absence of disease; nor is fitness just about how you look. We practice healthy habits daily to connect deeper with the source of our strength, power, creativity, and vitality.

When you push your body beyond what is comfortable, you expand your energy capacity. Add to that eating high quality, nutrient-dense whole foods and you have the building blocks for creating robust, physical health. *It is very difficult to achieve a high level of vitality without good physical health.*

Good physical health gives us the energy to be more active, present and engaging. This in turn attracts others to us and assists in further bolstering health. In fact, research has shown that regular positive human interactions help to boost our immunity.

I'm assuming that you're reading this book because you're interested in ways to energize your life. If this is the case, you're not going to be successful unless you achieve some degree of physical vitality.

Physical vitality is the foundation upon which all the other pillars rest.

It shapes your daily mental, emotional and spiritual experiences. Without it, you lack focus and concentration. You feel irritable, impatient, overwhelmed and insecure more easily. It is also easier to become disconnected from your true mission and purpose.

Phillip G. is a highly respected forty-one-year-old vice president of an international medical devices company. He's married and has a two-year-old son. When I sat down with Phillip exactly one year ago, he was spending two weeks in town, then three weeks on airplanes travelling to several Latin American countries; negotiating million dollar contracts with high level government officials and hospital executives.

He sat down across from me, slouching in his chair. Shoulders rolled forward. Barely making eye contact as we spoke. Here in front of me was a very powerful business executive who made millions of dollars for his company, and was paid very well for his efforts. Yet, he looked completely dejected — like a man who had lost sight of what's truly important to him. So, he slogged through his day, hoping his busy schedule would distract him from the great void he felt in his life.

"I can't continue like this," he said. "I'm killing myself. I barely have time to spend with my wife and newborn son because I'm always on the road. I'm always tired and I feel like crap because I'm constantly on the run, grabbing a bite to eat where I can and never having time to exercise. I can't go on like this."

Fortunately for Phillip, he got tired of his wife nagging him to make a change, so he finally stopped long enough to reflect on his life. He used to love his job, but his priorities were different now with a newborn baby in the house.

"I would like to be around to see my son grow up and have the energy to play with him, instead of being tired all the time," he said.

"I want my life back. I want to feel strong, confident and alive again."

Phillip's situation is not all that uncommon. Every week I get several emails from busy people all over the world who are pretty much saying the same thing.

They're tired and over-committed, but they know that there's got to be another way.

The good news is that there is.

You don't have to let your circumstances dictate your life. You can take back your power.

You can cultivate physical vitality.

You can energize your life and feel alive again.

7 Ways to Cultivate Physical Vitality

1. Get your million-dollar body back

What is your body worth? How much money would you pay for it? Of course, this depends on whom you ask.

I posed this question a few years ago to one of my private clients who was on the waiting list for a new lung, and she replied that she would give up all her possessions and be in debt for several lifetimes for the opportunity to breathe again without the assistance of an oxygen tank.

But if your body is worth so much, why do so many of us neglect and abuse it? Or as Jon Gordon put it in his book, Energy Addict:

> *"We take better care of our $20,000 cars than our priceless bodies.
> We don't exercise our million-dollar body because we have to
> work fifteen hours a day at our $60,000 a year job."*

But know this: it's never too late to start taking positive steps that will help to energize your life.

Good health is the foundation for reaching your highest vision. Without it, your *attention will be scattered, your mind unfocused, and your energy wasted* on recovery efforts.

When the body is healthy, fit and strong, you have more energy for your daily pursuits. You also tend to be more present and engaging when you're not burdened by what ails you. Like the old saying goes, "when your shoes fit comfortably, you no longer think about your feet."

So, how do you get your body back?

First, work on improving your health. Next, strive to attain a higher level of fitness. Finally, challenge yourself to build your leanest body ever.

Improving your health is very simple. Just incorporate more physical activity into your day and change one meal each week to include the healthiest sources of unprocessed whole foods.

Any activity that elevates your heart rate is great for your health. Try brisk walking, jogging, swimming, biking, hiking, yoga, Pilates, or even dancing. Learning a new sport, like tennis, is also a great way to stay active and get healthier. Weight training is also necessary to improve your lean body mass and for increasing your bone density.

Remember, a healthy lifestyle isn't a destination; it is a journey you take daily through the choices you make. So, choose to eat more unprocessed whole foods such as fish, chicken, eggs, tofu, whole grains, legumes, fruits, vegetables, berries, and healthy plant-based fats (avocado, nuts, seeds, extra virgin olive oil).

For help with your meal plan, pick up a copy of one of my books, *Dr. Del's Rapid Fatloss Meal Plan, or 10-Minute Meals*.

After you've successfully developed a healthy lifestyle, it's time to take your fitness to the next level. Like life, if you're going to get your body back, you're going to have to challenge your assumptions of what you think is possible for yourself.

Can you look good naked at any age? Absolutely yes! I've worked with clients in their sixties and seventies to help them get fitter, stronger, leaner and healthier than they were in their forties and fifties. This is also possible for you if you're willing to work for it.

The entire process of building great health and transforming your body is outlined in my last series of books, *Dr. Del's Rapid Fatloss Program*, which is a series of four books. You can learn more about these at my website *drdelmillers.com*.

2. Do something you love

It's been twenty years since I first started playing tennis and back in the early days, I used to practice with a few older guys in the neighborhood park. My favorite guy was Jack, an eighty-two year old Chinese guy. Jack was unusual for his age. He was fit, agile, and he moved around the court better than the other guys who were twenty years his junior.

The thing I remember most about Jack, though, was his laugh. Jack was a very happy guy who loved playing tennis. I got the feeling that he was just happy being there. I can only imagine how invigorating it must feel to still have the physical capability to do something you love even in your twilight years.

Think about it. *When do you feel most alive?* Is it when you're doing things that you have to do? Or is it when you're pursuing your passions? When you can totally lose yourself in the dance of the activity that hours seem like mere minutes.

I've traveled all over the world and the people I've met who've been the most alive and vital are those who regularly engage in activities just for the love of it. They played sports, danced, worked in their gardens, or just sat and read a book with a cup of tea. It doesn't seem to matter what they do. What matters is that they do something just for the shear joy of it.

So remember, the simplest way to enhance your physical vitality and therefore your energy is *to make time for joy.*

3. Lose your mind and come to your senses

In our hyper-connected world we often feel overwhelmed, distracted and pre-occupied with the myriad of thoughts in our heads. When we're not busy thinking and worrying about what was supposed to happen and what may or may not happen, we're running through all the items on our "to do" list and worrying how on earth we're going to get them all done.

Unfortunately, such mental masturbation is very draining. The constant mental chatter not only robs us of vital energy, it also prevents us from being present and fully engaged.

To learn to quiet your "monkey mind," spend *ten minutes a day in complete silence* where you won't be interrupted. You can do this in your office peering out the window, at the beach, at the park, or sitting on a bench in the middle of the city.

You don't need to do anything special. Just sit quietly and allow your thoughts to pass like words on a screen. Over time, your mind will generate fewer thoughts and you will become more acutely aware of what you're seeing, hearing, smelling and feeling instead.

Another excellent practice to help you get out of your head is to *commit your thoughts to paper.* Write down your daily activities on your calendar and cross them off as they are completed. Transfer those that you didn't get to over to another day.

I would also encourage you to keep an idea journal close by where you can write down ideas as they come into your mind. The act of writing not only clears your mind, it helps to keep you focused on doing something in the present.

Why do you want to lose your mind and come to your senses? Well, *we rarely spend time thinking about what is happening in the present.* Instead, most of our thoughts are about the past or the future.

And since thoughts are energy, we're expending a lot of energy thinking about things that we cannot control. Spending a few minutes each day just observing and interacting with our environment — seeing the sights, smelling the smells, hearing the sounds, and feeling the air caressing our skin — will release a lot of "trapped" mental energy and leave us feeling refreshed and reinvigorated.

4. Limit your interactions with the "energy suckers"

Daily, most of us allow others to steal our vital energy. We allow coworkers, family members and friends to slowly drain our energy with their negative attitudes and constant demands on our time and attention.

These are the people I call the "energy suckers."

They're energy suckers because our interactions with them leave us drained physically, mentally, emotionally and spiritually. When we associate with them regularly, instead of feeling inspired to see them, we end up feeling sad and wilted like a plant that hasn't been watered in a while.

Of course it may not always be possible to dictate who shows up in our work environment or with whom we have to associate during our workday. However, *we do have control over how we allow them to affect us.*

Another less recognized aspect of the "energy sucker syndrome" is the "energy martyrdom complex." People with this issue just can't say no. They commit to more than they can handle, and then silently feel bitter and angry with themselves.

A good example of this is the mom who can't say "no" to her kids, or the employee who can't say "no" to her boss. She commits herself to much more than she can handle and is silently bitter over her inability to say no.

A simple solution to the energy martyrdom complex is to plan ahead and commit your daily tasks to your calendar. When something new comes up, as is often the case, first decide if it goes to the top, middle or bottom of your priority list.

The reason why energy martyrs get bitter at themselves is because they often commit to doing new lower priority tasks ahead of the high priority items on their list.

When you learn to take charge of your time, instead of allowing others to dictate how you spend it, you will plug an important "energy leak" that drains your daily reserves.

5. Get connected; find your tribe

Strong social relationships affect all aspects of our health. Studies show that social relationships have both short and long-term effects on our immune, metabolic, cardiovascular, and nervous systems.

These studies consistently show that *individuals who are more socially connected are healthier and may live longer than their more isolated peers.*

Strong social ties also reduce mortality risk among those with documented medical conditions. For instance, among adults with coronary artery disease, the socially isolated had a risk of subsequent cardiac death two-and-a-half times greater than their more socially connected peers.

In fact, a number of these studies have found compelling evidence linking a low quantity or quality of social ties with a host of conditions, including development and progression of cardiovascular disease, recurrent heart attacks, atherosclerosis, reduced immunity, high blood pressure, cancer and delayed cancer recovery, and slower wound healing.

It doesn't matter what type of social relationships you develop. What matters most is the human connection and interaction that takes place within your community, large or small. It could be a religious community, social club, or just an informal group of friends and relatives that you regularly commune with.

The best way to "find your tribe," is to connect with others who share your passions. What is it that you love to do? Do you love to dance, garden, read books, or are you a connoisseur of fine restaurants? Whatever it is that you love to do, connect with those who share your passion. Chances are, there are already thriving communities of people out there who share your passion.

As a youngster growing up in New York City, my tribe was the martial arts community. I developed close friendships with people I took classes with. We competed in martial arts tournaments together. We had frequent social and holiday gatherings. We were and still are a family thirty years later.

When I moved to Los Angeles, skate dancing at Venice Beach became my new passion. So I joined the community of skate dancers. We danced together every weekend. We had regular parties and annual summer camping trips. This tight-knit group of skate dancers became my new family.

A few years later Ballroom Latin and salsa dancing became my new passion. And of course, there are already thriving communities of dancers all over the world. I've made lasting friendships with other dancers on my visits to Australia, Japan, Sweden, Brazil, and dozens of cities around the US.

It isn't difficult to find your tribe. All you have to do is follow your passion. When you do, you will connect deeply with other like-minded souls. Your new tribe will become your new community and from that community, you will have a chance to cultivate the richest possible relationships with a few of your fellow passion seekers.

Your new tribe will lead you to your new family and the strong social ties you develop within that family will enhance your physical vitality beyond measure and make you feel alive.

6. Get back to nature

Are you an indoor zombie suffering from nature deficiency? Unfortunately, our modern lifestyle keeps many of us indoor all day, breathing stale re-circulated air and exposed to a variety of the toxic chemicals in office buildings.

This is bad news for one's health because nature deficiency can suppress immune systems and sharply increase the risk for illness and disease.

Consider this: a landmark 1984 study published in the journal Science found that hospital surgical patients who had a view out a window, or just a view of a nature-scene photograph, healed faster, had shorter hospital stays, and required less pain medication.

Now if just a view out the window or looking at a photograph of nature could have such a dramatic effect on surgical patients, imagine the impact that actually taking a walk in nature could have on one's well-being.

Another study published in the journal Applied Psychology found that children diagnosed with ADHD, (Attention Deficit Hyperactivity Disorder) who regularly played in outdoor settings with lots of green grass and trees have milder ADHD symptoms than those who played indoors.

Getting back to nature doesn't just make you feel better, it is also very healing. For example, a walk in the woods has been demonstrated to lead to an increase in your body's level of "natural killer" cells; an important part of the body's immune response to cancer. This happens because plants emit a chemical called phytoncides that protects them from rotting and insects. When you take a walk in the woods you breathe in this plant chemical, giving your immune system a boost.

Here are a few simple ways to get back to nature:
- Have a picnic in the park at lunchtime
- Take a walk outside while returning your phone calls
- Take a hike in the woods with family or friends as a weekly ritual
- Have a walking meeting outside instead of sitting in a conference room

Getting back to nature will not only enhance your physical vitality, it helps you connect at a much deeper spiritual level.

7. Make time for rest and renewal

Most people underestimate the impact that rest and renewal have on our health, energy, and daily ability to perform at our best. In fact, as a society, we don't value regular renewal.

In business, those who "burn the midnight oil" are looked upon as the go-getters; the one's who should be emulated. Never mind that over the past thirty years the research has been very conclusive that a good night's sleep — followed by intermittent daily breaks — is vital for health, productivity, and personal fulfillment.

One such study published in *Sleep Medicine Reviews* journal demonstrated definitively that consistent sleep deprivation affects more than just our mental faculties.

Chronic sleep deprivation can decrease insulin sensitivity, increase appetite, and reduce the body's total energy expenditure. In other words, skimping on your sleep regularly can lead to obesity and escalate your chances for developing diabetes.

Another study published in the *Annals of Internal Medicine*, reported that research subjects who slept only four hours a night for two nights had an 18 percent decrease in leptin, a hormone that tells the brain there is no need for more food, a 28 percent increase in ghrelin, a hormone that triggers hunger, and a 24 percent increase in appetite.

Study participants also reported a surge in desire for sweets, such as candy and cookies, salty foods such as chips and nuts, and starchy foods such as bread and pasta. In short, *long-term sleep deprivation can increase your chances of gaining weight.*

The research is very clear that sleeping less than seven hours a night negatively affects health, energy and quality of work. Furthermore, what we do to renew our energy during the day is just as important.

In the 1960's sleep research pioneer Nathaniel Kleitman discovered what he called the Basic Rest Activity Cycle (BRAC) during sleep. It is a biological cycle during which we go through the five stages of sleep. A decade later he reported that we go through the same 90-120 minute cycle during the day.

When we're awake, our brainwaves are faster during the first half of the BRAC cycle, so we feel focused and alert. Our brainwaves gradually slow during the second half until we reach the final twenty minutes when we feel tired and a bit dreamy.

What Dr. Kleitman's research suggests is that it is best to go through two-hour periods during the day of focused dedicated work, followed by a period of rest or a break. A renewal break gives the body a chance to recharge and re-energize.

However, instead of taking a true renewal break, most of us try to override our body's natural ultradian rhythm with sugar and caffeine. This is counterproductive because it puts the body in a fight-or-flight mode with elevated levels of the stress hormones adrenalin and cortisol.

When this happens, the prefrontal cortex area of the brain that is responsible for creativity begins to slowly shut down. The end result is that we become more impulsive and reactive. This is not the prescription for creative problem solving.

Instead of overriding your body's natural signals with stimulants, take a true renewal break at two-hour intervals throughout the day. Leave whatever it is you're doing and take a walk, stretch, or have a conversation with someone.

To enhance your physical vitality and the quality of your energy throughout the day, you must learn to respect the body's circadian and ultradian rhythms. Sufficient sleep at night (7-8 hours) and regular renewal breaks throughout the workday, will help you to be fully engaged and bring your best to whatever you do.

Physical Vitality Action Plan

A body that is healthy, fit, and strong is the foundation for physical vitality.

Step 1: **Get your body back**

- Move more. **Get out and walk, bike, jog, hike, dance, swim, or take up a new sport** like tennis. It doesn't matter what you do, just do it at least three days per week. Add some weight training at least a couple times per week to build lean muscle.
- *Eat well*. **Eat whole foods that are minimally processed or not at all.** Again, the whole process of what to eat and how to train to get your body back is outlined in *Dr. Del's Rapid Fatloss Program*, a series of four books.

Step 2: **Make time for joy**

Do something regularly that make your heart sing (tennis, dance, gardening, reading, etc.).

- **What is your joy activity and what would you have to give up in order to make time for it at least once per week?**

Step 3: **Find your tribe**

Strong social relationships are good for your health and longevity.

- **Which community of people share your passion?** Where are they?

Step 4: **Make time for daily renewal**

- **Take a "true" break from whatever you're doing every two hours**, even for just five minutes.

Get Exclusive Extras at *EnergizedLifeAcademy.com*

~ **Energize Your Life Action Plan workbook**

~ **7 Questions (to Ask Yourself) to Help You
Fuel Your Life with Purpose, Passion & Play ebook**

~ **Free coaching videos on all seven pillars**

Energize Your Life

Become a Conduit for Positive Energy

*"Positive energy attracts.
Negative energy repels."*
— Del Millers

Pillar #4: Positive Energy

It was December 2013, and I was flying home to Los Angeles from Charlotte, NC via Chicago O'Hare airport. Unfortunately, flying through Chicago in the winter during bad weather automatically spells delays and canceled flights. And that was exactly the case. The flight that was supposed to leave before mine from Chicago to Los Angeles was canceled. And so was mine.

Imagine being one of those American Airline attendants that night trying his or her best to accommodate 300 angry, stranded passengers.

But, as I stood in line that night waiting my turn to talk to the attendant, I made a radical decision to adopt a positive outlook about my situation. I had every right to be as pissed off as everybody else in that terminal, but I chose instead to focus on one thought to the exclusion of all others: "I am on the next flight to Los Angeles."

I kept repeating that one single thought in my head over and over again with a single mindedness of purpose. I would also look at the attendant every so often and send her a silent message — "you've got a seat for me on that next plane, I know it."

By the time I reached the counter, I was told that the next flight was fully booked. I looked at the attendant with a smile and said, "rough night isn't it, Nancy?"

"You have no idea," she replied with a sigh.

Then with a smile I said "Nancy, I know you're probably all booked up, but I've got an event in Los Angeles tomorrow and I'm the keynote speaker, so I would be forever grateful if you could somehow get me on the next flight out tonight."

She said, "Mr. Millers we're all booked up, but please have a seat and I will see what I can do."

Fifteen minutes later, I was standing in line with a boarding pass in hand, waiting to board my flight to Los Angeles.

Yes, I know the pessimists would say that I just got lucky. But did I?

Or did I create the right conditions that led the universe to conspire in my favor?

The truth is, I don't know. All I know is that I was sitting on the next flight home while most of the angry people were on their way to a hotel for the night.

Here's what I do know for sure.

My positive optimistic attitude allowed me to stop thinking about myself long enough to empathize with Nancy's situation. When I said to Nancy, "rough night, isn't it?" I genuinely meant it, and she felt that.

Here's something else I do know for sure.

When you go out of your way to put yourself in the other person's shoes and see things from their perspective, it often creates a win-win situation. You'll find that most people will go out of THEIR way to accommodate your needs.

Now, I don't know what exactly Nancy did that night to get me a seat on that last flight out of Chicago to Los Angeles, but I'm certain she went out of her way to accommodate me.

Why would she do that?

Positive energy attracts positive results and people to you. Negative energy repels.

There's a lot of negativity in the world. We are surrounded by it. It's inescapable. You hear about it every time you turn on the television. It's thrown in your face when you walk out the door and have to listen to your neighbor complaining about how much he hates his dead end job. Again!

The world is filled with negative energy because it boosts television ratings and helps to sell newspapers and magazines. Negative energy is controversial, provocative, and confrontational. Just watch an episode of most Reality TV and you'll see what I mean.

Positive energy, on the other hand, is subtle, purposeful, and uplifting. It's the kind of energy that gives you the momentum you need to move in the direction of a larger vision for your life.

Positive energy is like a magnet. It attracts positive people and positive results into your life.

But how can you become a conduit for positive energy in a world obsessed with sensationalism, controversy, and fear?

You cultivate positive energy by taking positive actions every day. Or as Jon Gordon puts it in his book, The Energy Bus, you must "feed positive dog:"

A man goes to the village to visit the wise man and he says to the wise man, "I feel like there are two dogs inside me. One dog is positive, loving, kind, and gentle dog and then I have this angry, mean-spirited and negative dog and they fight all the time. I don't know which is going to win." The wise man thinks for a moment and he says, "I know which is going to win. The one you feed the most, so feed positive dog."

7 Ways to Cultivate Positive Energy Everyday

1. Be Happy

Talking about happiness is like talking about love. You choose to be happy just the same way you choose to love. Neither depends on what you have or don't have, or how much crap you've got going on in your life at the moment. *Happiness is a choice.*

To be happy, just keep moving towards the light. In other words, find ways to embrace and enhance the positives in your life, even in your darkest hour.

2. Laugh Often

Have you noticed that it's impossible to remain in a negative mood when you're laughing? That's because *laughter is the gateway to happiness.* So the moment you start laughing you will automatically put yourself in your 'happy place'.

Laughter fills you with positive energy that affects all four dimensions of the human experience—physical, mental, emotional, and spiritual.

So everyday give yourself permission to have a few good belly laughs. It's okay; you'll feel more energized and alive. Personally, I like to watch an old episode or two of Seinfeld before going to bed. That way, I'll forget all about the troubles of the day and laugh myself right to sleep.

3. Look a Stranger in the Eyes, Smile, and Say Hello

Most of us walk around each day completely unaware of what's happening around us. We go out of our way not to make eye contact or to engage with others. While such "stranger anxiety" behavior is often rationalized as a safety precaution, the end result is that we miss important opportunities to enhance our own positive energy.

When was the last time you looked a stranger in the eyes, smiled, and said "hello?" What about your neighbor, or even the people you see on the elevator everyday?

The simple act of looking someone in the eyes and smiling when you greet them may not seem like such a big thing to you, but it may mean a world of difference to the other person. To them the fact that you acknowledged their presence may help them to feel "seen" instead of feeling invisible.

A few years ago I was walking to my car after a tennis game in the park. As I was walking down the narrow path that led to the parking lot, I stopped to let an elderly lady go by. She was walking very slowly with a cane and looked rather melancholy. For the sake of argument, I'll call her Grandma Betty, since I don't recall her name.

But as Grandma Betty walked by, I looked at her with a big smile and said, "Good morning, how are you today?" She looked up at me with the biggest smile and said, "young man, you have just made my day." She said, "I don't move like I used to anymore and since my husband died, I don't get to talk to too many people either, because everyone is always in a hurry."

Ten minutes later as we said our goodbyes, Grandma Betty was no longer looking at the ground while she was walking. She walked away smiling, her eyes gazing about as if she had a renewed vigor to engage with the world again.

That's what happens when you share positive energy, you never know how it's going to affect others. But sharing also impacts your own energy. It enhances your positive mood and makes you feel more connected to humanity.

At least, that's how I felt as a walked back to my car after my encounter with Grandma Betty.

4. Be optimistic when you have every reason to be pessimistic

It's easy to have positive energy when things are going right and everything is unfolding as they should. But the time when you need positive energy the most is when your world is filled with negativity, when everything that can go wrong is going wrong, and when you're surrounded by negative people and negative results.

This is when you really need to dig down deep and find the source of your inspiration and reconnect with your larger vision. If you don't, you'll be buried alive in the pit of despair alongside all the other negative people who pulled you in.

5. Redirect Negative Energy

The world is filled with negativity and an important skill to learn is how to redirect, or as we say in tai chi practice, ward-off, incoming negative energy.

It's impossible to shut yourself off from negative people because we live, work and socialize with them. So a good practice is to learn to redirect their negative energy. How do you do that? *Simply change the energetic of the conversation or change the conversation itself.*

For instance, if someone is bitching about their life, instead of joining the pity party, simply point out some of the positives of their situation. Or you might simply say, "Oh, before I forget, I've been meaning to ask you…" Then ask them a question about something positive and uplifting. You take control of the situation and completely redirect the energy of the conversation.

6. Embrace Negative Emotions

Keep in mind that sometimes the biggest negative energy sucker in your life is you! In this case, it's important that you learn to embrace, that's right, embrace your negative emotions. Emotions have both a positive and a negative charge. Unfortunately, quite often, negative emotions can easily spiral out of control and take you down a very dark and lonely path.

However, the more you resist not feeling the way you do, the longer you will keep yourself trapped in that negative state. The fastest way to transform negative emotions is to go through them as quickly as possible.

That is, if you feel pissed off at the world, find a constructive way of getting as angry as you can. Feel like hitting something? Go hit a pillow, punching bag, or get a stick and take a few whacks at a tree (one that you can't possibly hurt).

Of course, dealing with emotions is never an easy thing. It requires a degree of emotional intelligence and self-awareness. But start practicing with the small stuff, like simple everyday annoyances, and eventually you will develop a degree of emotional sophistication that will serve you well.

7. Embrace "Necessary Endings"

In the wise words of the Oracle from The Matrix movies, "Everything that has a beginning must come to an end."

Yes, sometimes it is necessary to end some relationships for the good of your own personal evolution. These "necessary endings" are never easy. Sometimes they're even very painful. Nevertheless, they're quite necessary for the highest good of all concerned.

Keeping negative people in your immediate sphere of influence will be toxic to your energy level. They will also slow you down from achieving anything positive and worthwhile in your life. Sometimes you have to release negative people from your life in order to create space for others who will support and encourage you.

This is also the case for those projects and long-term commitments that have turned into energy suckers. If your commitments don't bring energy to your life, it's time to let them go. So don't be afraid to embrace these "necessary endings." You'll be glad you did.

Positive Energy Action Plan

You cultivate positive energy by taking positive action.

Step 1: **Laugh often**

- **How can you put more laughter into your life** (favorite TV show, cartoon, joke of the day, etc.)?

Step 2: **Share your positive energy**

- **Who can you share your positive energy with** on a daily basis

Step 3: **Redirect negative energy**

- **Who are the negative people in your life** who constantly bring you down?
- **How can you redirect their negative energy?**

Step 4: **Embrace your negative emotions**

- Instead of acting out, **what can you do when you feel mad at the world?**

Step 5: **Necessary endings**

- Are there any **relationships, projects, or bad habits in your life that are sucking your energy** like a vampire?
- **What do you need to do to get rid of them?**

Get Exclusive Extras at *EnergizedLifeAcademy.com*

~ **Energize Your Life Action Plan workbook**

~ **7 Questions (to Ask Yourself) to Help You
Fuel Your Life with Purpose, Passion & Play ebook**

~ **Free coaching videos on all seven pillars**

Energize Your Life

Practice Positive Psychology

*"The greatest discovery of my generation
is that a human being can alter his life by
altering his attitudes of mind."*
— *William James*

Pillar #5: Positive Psychology

Human beings are very complex creatures. We operate in four dimensions of reality – physical, mental, emotional, and spiritual.

For years we have been taught that these four dimensions of the human experience are separate from each other. However, most of us know that they're all interrelated, and science is finally confirming that fact.

Here's the truth: the way we think about our health, stress, life's daily setbacks, or a momentous defeat affects us more significantly than the events themself. And research has shown that although our brain controls our biochemistry, our thoughts control the brain.

Today, the field of behavioral medicine is based on studies showing that anxiety, depression and stress show up in the body as physical symptoms and can cause the same harm as germs, unhealthy lifestyle, or damaged cells.

Other fields like psychoneuroimmunology study how our daily stressors — and the negative emotions associated with them — translate into physical changes within the body.

For example, the brain controls our immune function via a system of hormones. And research has shown that stress and negative emotions can significantly increase the secretion of some of these hormones (cortisol and adrenaline), which can increase the risk of infection and delay the healing process.

On the other hand, exercise, meditation, self-hypnosis, and other relaxation techniques can cause the brain to release hormones that improve the body's immune function and reduce inflammation.

Research has also widely documented that most drugs work on the placebo effect. In one such study, brain-imaging of Parkinson's disease patients given a fake drug showed that they were producing equivalent amounts of the "muscle-controlling chemical acetylcholine as were the patients receiving the real medication."

- The brain is a chemical factory
- The brain operates on chemicals called "neurotransmitters." These neurotransmitter chemicals have the ability to produce different emotional states.
- The most widely researched of these neurotransmitters are serotonin, dopamine, norepinephrine, and endorphins.

The levels of these chemicals *regulate everything* from your *mood, cravings,* various *physical symptoms* (such as movement disorders in Parkinson's patients caused by abnormally low levels of dopamine), *physical energy*, and levels of *pain.*

The really interesting thing here is that your thoughts can change your brain chemistry and how neurotransmitters function...as in the following examples by psychologist, Dr. Joe Carter:

> *"If a man walks into a room with a gun, we think 'threat', and the brain releases norepinephrine. We become tense, alert, develop sweaty palms, and our heart beats faster. If he then bites the barrel of the gun, telling us the gun is actually chocolate, the brain rapidly changes its opinion and we relax and laugh – the joke's on us."*

Practice Positive Psychology

You feel what you think! Positive thinking works. As the above example suggests, what you think about a situation actually creates your mood.

> *"Passed over for a promotion, you can either think you'll never get ahead in this job (lowering serotonin and making us depressed) or assume that you are being held back for another promotion or job transfer (makes a better mood)."*

The fact is negative thoughts affect your brain in such a way that produces negative emotions. And positive thoughts lead to better health, more energy, and a greater degree of resilience that helps you bounce back from setbacks.

So how can you train your mind to produce more positive results in your health, your relationships, at work— in your overall experience of life?

Practice positive psychology.

Unlike traditional psychology's preoccupation with what's wrong with people, the emphasis of positive psychology is what goes right with people.

What are the factors that make life truly worth living? And can this new science be taught as a set of skills that we all can learn to significantly improve our lives?

As you learn to master some of the skills of positive psychology (such as positive emotions, flexible optimism, and active behavior, as outlined below) and incorporate them into your daily routines, you will energize your life.

> *"One small positive thought this morning can change your whole day."*
> *– Unknown*

7 Simple Brain Hacks for Increasing Your Positive Energy

1. Fail your way to success

I started playing tennis again on Sunday mornings after a five-year hiatus. Tennis can be a very frustrating sport because it requires both skill and timing that come only through regular practice.

Of course, when you haven't played for a while, you're going to make quite a few errors. This gets very frustrating and like most of the other guys on the court, I developed a very bad habit. Every time I made an error, I would berate myself and say very nasty and negative things to myself.

Things like, "Why are you so stupid?" Or "You stupid son of a b****, how could you miss such an easy shot?"

Unfortunately, this negative self-talk contributed only to my defeat because the more I berated myself, the worse I would end up playing.

So I decided to try a new strategy. Why not bring my thirty years of martial arts practice with me onto the tennis court? I told myself to forget about winning or losing. Just play the game and work at getting better at something each time I step on the court.

I also adopted a new positive mindset and a couple of new positive self-talk mantras to say to myself after I make a mistake. If I hit the ball out, I would say to myself, "That's okay, it was a lovely shot, just a little wide, that's all. I'll get the next one."

Practice Positive Psychology

Or before I serve, I would say to myself, "Just one serve could change the course of this game. Just one serve."

So, did my new positive mindset make a difference in my game?

It made all the difference in the world.

In the last four months, my game progressed four times faster than the previous four months. But more importantly, when I step onto the court now my only objective is to play inspired.

The really interesting thing is, the more I encourage myself after making an error, the better I end up playing. So I no longer curse myself after making errors.

Unfortunately, responding to life's challenges with a positive attitude is not the norm. Most of us react negatively to our setbacks.

Martin Seligman, one of the founders of the positive psychology movement and author of Learned Optimism, coined the phrase "learned helplessness" to describe the extremely negative reaction that most people have when bad things happen to them.

According to Dr. Seligman, "your way of explaining things to yourself determines how helpless you can become, or how energized, when you encounter everyday setbacks, as well as momentous defeats."

He calls this your "explanatory style," which is your habitual way of explaining bad events. As it turns out, the words we tell ourselves when we fail is a habitual pattern of thought learned in childhood. And directly related to how we see our place in the world.

Do you see yourself as "valuable and deserving," or "worthless and hopeless?"

So a negative explanatory style will contribute to helplessness, or the feeling that whatever you do doesn't really matter. This is the hallmark of pessimism.

People with negative explanatory styles often see their setbacks as permanent, pervasive, and personal. This means that simple failures can often lead to feelings of insecurity and depression for long periods of time.

When they fail they often say things like, "Diets never work," "I'm no good," "I'm stupid," or "I will never get it."

On the other hand, a positive explanatory style stops the feeling of helplessness. *People with a positive explanatory style are usually able to see setbacks as temporary.*

Because those with positive explanatory styles don't turn their failures into a personal condemnation of themselves, they're able to bounce back relatively quickly. Their mental resilience protects them against the feeling of helplessness that engulfs those with a negative explanatory style.

This feeling of helplessness is often what leads to severe depression.

As Dr. Seligman writes,

> *"Failure makes everyone at least momentarily helpless. It's like a punch in the stomach. It hurts, but the hurt goes away—for some people almost instantly...For others, the hurt lasts; it seethes, it roils, it congeals into grudge...They remain helpless for days or perhaps months, even after only small setbacks. After major defeats they may never come back."*

The good news is we can all change our explanatory styles. We can reprogram our subconscious minds to respond with optimism, which generates positive energy that leads to positive actions.

As usual, to create change you have to first become aware of how you respond to daily setbacks. Do you react with negativity and hopelessness? Or do you see your setbacks as temporary obstacles to overcome?

Keep in mind that you may be a very optimistic person in most areas of your life. However, as the old saying goes, "to know a person is to see him/her in action."

How do you respond to life's challenges in the heat of battle? What are you saying to yourself when you're competing and you're getting your butt kicked?

What are you saying to yourself when you have a work deadline to meet and everything that can go wrong is going wrong?

Becoming aware of the inner dialogue you're having with yourself when you fail is the first step in developing a positive explanatory style.

That's how I was able to change the negative dialogue I was having with myself during my tennis games. I literally stopped in the middle of a game and asked myself, "Why am I being like this? This isn't me."

But the sad truth is, no matter how enlightened you think you are, your subconscious mind will always show you exactly who you really are and that is a great thing because you can then reprogram your subconscious mind to respond differently.

How do you go about doing this?

Well, like I did during my tennis games, as soon as you are in a moment of failure, you have to change your thought process, which then changes both your emotional state and your behavior.

The easiest way I've found to do this is to develop what I call a positive mantra that you will use to replace the negative dialogue that usually takes place after your setbacks.

Remember my mantra? "That's okay, it was a lovely shot, just a little wide, that's all. I'll get the next one."

Or before I serve, I would say to myself, "Just one serve could change the course of this game. Just one serve."

This process works because it immediately replaces your subconscious mind's negative thought process with more positive input in the moment of failure, which changes your emotional state and, most importantly, your actions.

"What is crucial is what you think when you fail," according to psychologist Dr. Martin Seligman.

"Changing the destructive things you say to yourself when you experience the setbacks that life deals all of us is the central skill of optimism."

2. Increase your "daily diet" of positive emotions

"The mind is its own place,
and in itself can make a heaven of hell,
a hell of heaven." – John Milton

Imagine for a moment that you lived in the era of our hunter-gatherer ancestors. You're out in the forest hunting for food, when suddenly you realized that you're not alone. You're being stalked.

As you slowly turn to face your stalker, a death chill comes over you as you stare into the hungry eyes of a wild 500-pound female lion. You become frozen with fear as it sinks in that you, the hunter, have now become the hunted.

You break out in a cold sweat. Your palms become sweaty and your heart is pounding in your chest like an African drum. The only thought that comes to your mind is....Ruuuuuun!

Negative emotions and the brain

Fear, like anger, is a powerful emotion that triggers your brain to focus on one thing only, your survival. When you're experiencing fear, anger, and extreme stress, your brain is programmed to shut out the outside world and everything that is unrelated to your immediate survival.

Negative emotions prevent our brains from seeing all possible options, because they trigger survival instincts.

Now, I realize that in our modern society we don't have to worry about coming face-to-face with a wild lion. However, our bodies are still programmed to react the same way when under the duress of all negative emotions.

I'm sure you can remember having a fight with someone and so consumed by your anger that you were unable to focus on anything else for hours.

Or feeling so overwhelmed by all the things you had to do at work that you were unable to think clearly, or even figure out where to begin.

This is what negative emotions do. They trigger your brain to shut anything out unrelated to your immediate survival. They narrow your thinking and prevent you from seeing all possible options.

As University of North Carolina-Chapel Hill researcher and professor, Barbara Fredrickson, wrote in American Scientist:

> *"The negative emotions have an intuitively obvious adaptive value: In an instant, they narrow our thought-action repertoires to those that best promoted our ancestors' survival in life-threatening situations."*

Positive emotions and the brain

Positive emotions, on the other hand, change the way our brains work. They expand awareness, build trust, and lead to more creative connections and positive outcomes, such as better negotiations.

Through her research, *"The Broaden-and-Built theory of Positive Emotions,"* Barbara Fredrickson demonstrated that when we're experiencing positive emotions like joy, love, gratitude, and contentment, we will see more possibilities in our lives.

According to Dr. Fredrickson,

> *"Instead of solving problems of immediate survival, positive emotions solve problems concerning personal growth and development. Experiencing a positive emotion leads to states of mind and to modes of behavior that indirectly prepare an individual for later hard times."*

During her experiment, she divided her subjects into five groups. Group-1 was shown images to induce feelings of joy. Group-2 induced feelings of contentment. Group-3, the control group, was shown neutral images that induced no particular emotion.

The last two groups (group-4 four and group-5) were shown clips to induce negative emotions (fear and anger, respectively).

After watching the clips, each participant was then given a blank sheet of paper with twenty lines and asked to imagine themselves in a situation where similar feelings would arise, then write down what they would do.

Groups four and five who saw clips of fear and anger had the fewest responses. The first two groups who saw clips of joy and contentment had a significantly higher number of responses, even compared to the control group.

Dr. Fredrickson's experiment was one of the first to clearly demonstrate that when you're experiencing positive emotions like joy and contentment, your mind will expand to explore new possibilities.

Bring your doctor candy

In another experiment performed by Alice Isen and her colleagues at Cornell University, the clinical reasoning of practicing physicians was tested. They induced the feeling of joy in some of the physicians with a small bag of candy; then asked all of them to solve a case of a patient with liver disease.

The result:

> *"The physicians who felt good were faster to integrate case information and less likely to become anchored on initial thoughts or come to premature closure in their diagnosis."*

Can positive emotions "undo" the effects of negative emotions?

Barbara Fredrickson's groundbreaking research on positive emotions clearly demonstrates that while negative emotions narrow people's mindset, positive emotions broaden them.

But, her work went even a step further. She was also able to demonstrate that *"positive emotions undo the lingering effects of negative emotions."*

In yet another experiment, participants were told that they had one minute to prepare a speech that would be videotaped and evaluated. This task induced feelings of anxiety, increased heart rate, blood vessel constriction, and elevated blood pressure (adverse cardiovascular activity).

Participants were then randomly assigned to view one of four films. The first two films elicited the positive emotions amusement and contentment. The third film served as the control neutral condition, and the fourth elicited feelings of sadness.

The cardiovascular activity of the first two groups who watched the positive-emotion films recovered sooner (returned to normal) than the neutral control group. The group that watched the sad film showed the most delayed recovery.

According to Dr. Fredrickson,

> "Because the positive emotions broaden people's thought-and- action repertoires, they may also loosen the hold that negative emotions gain on both mind and body, dismantle preparation for specific action and undo the physiological effects of negative emotions."

Where do you go from here?

Start working on your "positivity ratio." Fredrickson's research suggests that "we need at least three positive emotions to lift us up for every negative emotion that drags us down."

So make time on a daily basis to experience *love, joy, wonder, laughter,* and *gratitude*. Remember, such emotions are fleeting and may only last seconds or minutes. Nevertheless, they will expand your awareness, thinking, behavior, social connections, and your health.

What you do is up to you.

For me, I like to listen to really inspiring music when I do my daily cardio and weight training workouts. I also practice Tai chi, play tennis, hike, dance, and make time to just roll around on the floor with my three kids.

Sometimes I just stop what I'm doing for a few seconds to watch two squirrels chase each other up and down a tree or take a quick sniff of a beautiful flower as I'm passing by.

Again, what you do is up to you.

But as you can see, you can easily increase your daily "positivity ratio" just by getting in the habit of stealing little moments to experience love, joy, wonder, awe, playfulness, and a host of other positive emotions that will make you feel truly alive.

By the same token, don't beat yourself up when you experience negative emotions. They're a natural part of living; just work on getting through them as quickly as possible.

As we discussed earlier, the fastest way to recover from the affects of negative emotions is to experience positive emotions.

So, what positive emotion habits are you willing to cultivate in your life today?

3. Make stress your friend

Stress is good.

Your perception of stress is what determines whether it kills you or makes you stronger.

In the past ten years, the new science of stress has confirmed that people who experience significant stress, but don't perceive that stress as being bad for their health, live longer than those who experience the same level of stress and believe that stress is bad for you.

So as it turns out the new equation for stress is:

DS + PS = HO

Degree of Stress (DS) + Perception of Stress (PS) = Health Outcome (HO)

Fortunately or unfortunately, the most important factor in this equation is your perception of stress and not your degree of stress. The new science of stress tells us that *if you believe that stress is a bad thing it is*. But if you believe that stress is not a bad thing, it isn't.

The mind can be a powerful friend or foe. It all depends on your perceptions.

Unfortunately, I must confess that for the past twenty years, I, along with most other health and medical professionals, have been part of the problem.

We've been telling our clients and patients that stress is bad for their health. So instead of helping most of them to shape their health outcome for the better, we've done just the opposite.

Why do I believe that?

Most people live very stressful lives and the only other factor that determines whether that stress leads to a positive or adverse health outcome is their perception of stress.

And because, at the time, all the medical literature supported the point of view that stress response leads to anxiety, hypertension, and might even cause cardiovascular disease, that's the information we've been teaching people.

Unfortunately, we were wrong.

A 2013 TED talk by Kelly McGonigal turned me on to a number of fascinating new research studies on stress. These studies essentially demonstrated that stress isn't bad for your health. Our perception that stress is bad for our health is the real culprit.

Below is a brief overview of a couple of these studies.

The new science of stress

In a 2012 study published in Health Psychology, researchers at the University of Wisconsin-Madison, tracked 30,000 adults in the United States over an 8-year period.

Each participant was initially asked to rate his/her level of stress (a lot, moderate, a little, or almost none) over the previous year. Then, they were asked, do you believe that stress is harmful to your health?

Researchers then used public death records to find out who died after 8 years.

The participants who reported experiencing a lot of stress and who also believed that stress is harmful for your health had a 43% increased risk of dying.

On the other hand, those who experienced a lot of stress but didn't believe that stress is harmful were no more likely to die. In fact, they had the lowest risk of anyone in the study, including people who had relatively little stress.

Here's what the researchers had to say about the study:

> *"In this study, the perception that stress affects health was found to act synergistically with amount of stress to predict an increased risk of premature death. Specifically, reporting a lot of stress and perceiving that stress affected one's health a lot increased the risk of premature death by 43%."*

Harvard University's "Social Stress Test"

In this next study, conducted by researchers at Harvard University and published in the Journal of Experimental Psychology, I want you to imagine entering a room with strangers and being told that you're going to give a five-minute impromptu, videotaped speech on your personal weaknesses.

But to amp up your stress level, you're told that you will be evaluated on your performance and adding to your anxiety, throughout the speech, the evaluators provided negative feedback such as yawning, furrowed brow, crossed arms, frowning, etc.

Following the speech, you're also asked to perform an impromptu 5-min mental arithmetic task: Counting backward in steps of 7 from 996 while the evaluators provided negative feedback.

What do you think your normal physiological response would be in this situation?

For most of us, the normal stress response would be racing heartbeat, sweaty palms, elevated blood pressure, and we might even break out in a sweat. The typical stress response when we're stressed out. Sound familiar?

But here's where it gets really interesting.

Study participants were randomly assigned to 3 groups. Before the study, group-1 was told that the increased arousal (racing heartbeat, sweaty palms, elevated blood pressure, sweating) they might experience during stressful situations is not harmful.

"Instead, the instructions explained that our body's responses to stress have evolved to help us successfully address stressors and that increased arousal actually aids performance in stressful situations." In other words, these physical changes are a result of your body rising to the challenge to help you complete your task.

So instead of these physical changes being anxiety or a sign that you're not coping very well with the pressure, think of your increased heart rate and sweating as actually your body's way of energizing itself and supplying more oxygen to your brain to help you meet the challenge before you.

Group-2 was told "the best way to reduce nervousness and improve outcomes is to ignore the source of stress. Thus, they were told to look at an X placed to the left of the evaluators."

Group-3, the control group, wasn't given any special instructions.

Of the three groups, participants in group-1 were the least stressed out. They also had the most "improved cardiac efficiency." This means that their hearts were supplying more blood to their brains than was the case for the other two groups.

But, here's the most impressive result of the study.

Normally in situations when we're experiencing a threat or excessive stress, the body goes into "fight-or-flight" mode, which leads to constriction or narrowing of your blood vessels, limiting blood flow to the rest of the body. This is exactly what happens in the case of cardiovascular disease.

Participants in groups 2 and 3 experienced significant blood vessel constriction. However, those in group-1 did not. The blood vessels of participants in group-one remained relaxed.

By changing their perception of the stress response, group-1 participants were able to avoid the negative effects of stress that is often associated with cardiovascular disease.

So as it turns out, *stress can be your friend or your foe*.

Stress can make you stronger or it can kill you. It's all a matter of perspective.

So make stress your friend. How do you do that?

The next time you're in a really stressful situation, remember that your increased heart rate, sweaty palms and whatever else you feel is nothing more than your body's way of energizing you to rise to the challenge.

Focus on one thought at a time; then ask yourself, "What's next?"

You can handle it.

4. Increase your "active behavior"

How do you get ahead in the workplace of the future?

Whether you're a blue-collar worker, creative professional, executive, a self-employed individual, or entrepreneurial start-up, the workplace of the future is no longer local, it is global.

Because of global competition, technology and innovation, the workplace of tomorrow will require a greater degree of personal initiative.

In order to remain competitive in this new global marketplace, employees and self-employed individuals must take the initiative to constantly improve their knowledge and skills.

Studies of employees in different countries conducted by Michael Frese, a positive psychology researcher and professor of organizational psychology at Germany's University of Giessen, suggest that those who are most successful at work engage in a high degree of "active behavior."

Active behavior is comprised of three components: *self-starting, pro-active behavior*, and *persistence*.

According to Frese, self-starting behavior "implies that a person does something without being told, without getting an explicit instruction, or without an explicit role requirement."

For example, a blue-collar worker who takes the initiative to fix a broken machine even though it's not his job to do so. Or a secretary who takes the initiative to call around and find a better travel deal for the company than what was pre-negotiated.

Self-starting behavior means that somebody takes ownership of an idea, project or problem that is generally known but not acted upon.

Pro-active behavior means to anticipate problems and opportunities in the future and prepare to deal with them now.

And finally, when taking personal initiative, *persistence is often required in the face of professional obstacles*. Let's face it, people like their routines. So there is often pushback from co-workers or a superior when they're forced to abandon their routines and adapt to something new.

It takes persistence to persevere in the face of such obstacles.

Michael Frese's research, conducted in different countries and across various work environments, confirmed that those who engaged in active behavior often gain more empowerment and job satisfaction, and have greater control over their work. They also tend to change their work culture and environment for the better, and find new jobs easier if they become unemployed.

Where do you go from here?

Frese's research is based on "behaviors" that anyone can adapt to make their work more satisfying. It doesn't matter if you're an employee, executive, or self-employed.

These behaviors have been demonstrated to lead to optimal functioning at work. A high degree of pro-initiative in the work culture also equates to a higher level of innovation and change acceptance.

So how can you apply the three components of active behavior (self-starting, pro-active behavior, and persistence) to your current work situation?

5. Argue with yourself often

The mind can be a powerful friend or foe.

Over the past two decades, the science of positive psychology has clearly demonstrated that *we can improve our health and prolong our lives by changing the way we think.*

We know from the research that pessimists have more infectious illnesses and more doctor visits than optimists. Several studies have also confirmed that breast cancer survivors who approach their illness with an "optimistic fighting spirit" outlived those who were pessimistic about their condition.

How is any of this possible? And why is it that your psychological state is able to affect your physical body in such life-changing ways?

The answer is very simple. Your brain controls all the processes in your body, from your hormones to how well your immune system functions. However, your thoughts and emotions have corresponding brain states that control what the brain does.

In short, *your psychological state controls your brain. And your brain controls your physiology* — that's everything that happens in your body.

So, it is clear that you can improve your health, energize your life, and possibly add a few years to your life expectancy just by learning to deal with life's little challenges in a more positive way.

Instead of giving up or falling into deep depression, as most pessimists do, we learn to change our outlook about our problems and also change the conversations we have with ourselves.

After all, as Captain Jack Sparrow so eloquently said in the movie, *Pirates of the Caribbean:*

> *"The problem is not the problem. The problem is your attitude about the problem. Do you understand?"*

One of the most important tools in the positive psychology toolbox for helping us deal with problems in the moment is our ability to argue with ourselves.

Think about it. We argue with others all the time. So why not learn to argue with ourselves about the many inaccurate accusations we throw at ourselves daily, our negative reactions, and catastrophizing, that often turn out to be gross overreactions.

The A-B-C-D model

Psychologist Albert Ellis, the father of Rational Emotive Behavior Therapy (REBT), developed a simple A-B-C-D therapeutic model to help his patients deal with their emotional problems.

According to Dr. Ellis, when we encounter any form of adversity, we often react by thinking about it. Unfortunately, many of our beliefs have become habitual and are buried deep in our subconscious minds. Therefore, we're not even aware of them until we force ourselves to stop and focus on them.

The consequences of these beliefs show up as what we feel and do after experiencing adversity.

Therefore, *if we change our habitual beliefs that follow our setbacks, we will automatically change the outcome.*

So, how do you change a belief in the moment before it takes you down that destructive path of no return?

The first step in any process is always awareness. You have to practice recognizing what you're thinking when things go wrong. This is when it really matters.

To do so, try practicing the following exercise for a few days.

Whenever something upsets you, write down what it is (A = Adversity), your belief about what just happened (B = Belief), and how it made you feel or what did you do as a result of feeling that way (C = Consequence).

Adversity (A) – Belief (B) – Consequence (C)

Once you're aware of your negative beliefs, there are two ways to change them in the moment. The first is to "distract" yourself when they occur, by thinking about something else. Distraction techniques, such as slapping your palm hard against your desk while saying "STOP", or wearing a rubber band around your wrist and snapping it very hard, work well for immediate thought-interrupt.

The second way to change your beliefs is to "dispute" (D) them. *Disputing your beliefs is better for long-term results*.

To effectively dispute (D) a belief you have to go on the attack and argue with it the same way you would argue with someone with whom you strongly disagree.

To be effective in your arguments with yourself, you can point out evidence that contradicts your belief. For instance, most people who screw up on their diets after dieting diligently for, let's say, one month, usually fall into an automatic thought process that says "I'm weak and lack willpower."

However, if you've been able to maintain your diet for an entire month, you are not weak and you do not lack willpower. You just had a minor setback.

And since most events have many causes, you can also point out an alternative reason why it happened. For instance, if you've just had a fight with your spouse, instead of thinking "she's getting on my case again," you could think, "oh, well, she's just tired and hungry, that's all."

According to Dr. Martin Seligman,
> *"To dispute your own beliefs, scan for all possible contributing causes. Focus on the changeable...the specific...and the non-personal."*

This is the opposite of what most of us are used to doing. We've trained ourselves to go right to the worst-case scenario. Think about it. When you were in school and you were called to the principal's office, what was the first thought that came to your mind? "Uh, oh, what did I do wrong?" You probably had the same reaction when your boss told you that she would like to speak to you in her office.

Negative reactions come easier to most of us because we grew up around people who were conditioned to react this way, so this way of being is buried deep within our subconscious.

Arguing with yourself is an effective psychological tool for disputing and changing these negative beliefs.

But remember, *the two most important things to do when arguing with yourself is to point out evidence that is contrary to your held belief, and to focus on all other possible causes for what happened.* Look for things that are, as Dr. Seligman said, *"changeable, specific, and non-personal."*

6. Use "active constructive" responses to improve your relationships

When you fill your relationships with positive energy, you automatically energize your life. Not only is this very rewarding for you, but it also creates a situation where people love to be around you.

Did you know that the way you respond to others when they share good news with you could either build stronger relationships or tear them apart?

For decades Dr. Shelly Gable, associate professor of psychology at the University of California-Santa Barbara, has been studying what goes right in close relationships. Through her research, Dr. Gable found that how people respond to good news significantly predicts the quality of the relationship.

In fact, among couples, researchers can predict divorce within four years with 85%-90% accuracy, just by observing how they respond to each other.

Imagine for a second that your spouse, significant other, or close friend came home, or called you on the phone, beaming with excitement. "I just got promoted," she said.

According to Dr. Gable, you could respond in one of four ways:

1. Active constructive – "That's great, honey. You deserve it. I know it means a lot to you. Tell me what excites you most about it."

2. Active destructive – "I guess you'll be working more now? I can't believe they picked you."

3. Passive constructive – "Sounds good." Conveying no emotions.

4. Passive destructive – "What are we having for dinner?"

Of the four, only the "active constructive response" helps to reinforce close bonds while building trust and deeper intimacy between you.

This way of responding to others when they share good news also helps to magnify the uplifting effects of their good news because they feel supported.

On the other hand, a negative or semi-positive response to someone sharing good news could leave her feeling deflated and wishing she had never shared in the first place.

Why not give it a try with your friends, coworkers, or family? You don't need to do anything special, just be *genuinely interested and excited for the person sharing with you.*

Try asking them a little more about their good news (active) and build up the experience for them (constructive). In other words, just have them share more about what really excites them about their good news.

Practice this regularly in your relationships and you will fill your environment with positive energy. In fact, others will seek you out whenever they have something positive and exciting to share.

7. Practice "flexible optimism"

The optimist often sees the world, not as it is, but as it could be. The pessimist sees the world, not as it is, but as it might be.

Unfortunately, the pessimist often has his feet firmly planted on the ground, while the optimist is soaring above the clouds.

From this vantage point, it is the pessimist who resides closer to the present reality.

The optimist, through the power of the mind and the power of non-negative thinking, can change this reality. However, *sometimes it is important just to see the world as it is.*

If you're designing a new skyscraper or a bridge, these activities often call for a degree of mild pessimism. When lives are at stake, it is better to err on the side of safety and caution.

So sometimes the activity at hand may require that we invoke our inner pessimist in order to walk the line closest to reality.

I leave you with the words of Dr. Martin Seligman, the father of positive psychology:

> *"Pessimism has a role to play, both in society at large and in our own lives; we must have the courage to endure pessimism when its perspective is valuable. What we want is not blind optimism but flexible optimism – optimism with its eyes open. We must be able to use pessimism's keen sense of reality when we need it, but without having to dwell in its dark shadows."*

Positive Psychology Action Plan

Positive thoughts and emotions lead to positive actions.

Step 1: **What's your "explanatory style?"**
- For the next week, become aware of what you think or say to yourself immediately after a minor or major setback (at home, work or at play).
- How does it make you feel?
- If your thought process is negative, can you come up with a positive "mantra" to replace the negative input that you're feeding your subconscious mind?

Step 2: **Increase your "positivity ratio"**
- What specific things can you commit to today to experience simple little moments of love, joy, wonder, awe, or playfulness?

Step 3: **Make stress your friend**
- When you're experiencing the feeling of overwhelm (too much to do than you can possibly get done), how can you reframe your thoughts in a positive way that will serve you better?

Step 4: **Increase your "active behavior"**
- How can you apply the three components of active behavior (self-starting, pro-active behavior, and persistence) to your current work situation?

Step 5: **Practice arguing with yourself**
- Pick an upsetting event that happened recently. Write down what it is (A), your belief about what just happened (B), and how it made you feel or what did you do as a result of feeling that way (C). Next, dispute (D) your belief by pointing out evidence to the contrary.

Get Exclusive Extras at *EnergizedLifeAcademy.com*

~ **Energize Your Life Action Plan workbook**

~ **7 Questions (to Ask Yourself) to Help You Fuel Your Life with Purpose, Passion & Play ebook**

~ **Free coaching videos on all seven pillars**

Increase Your Prosocial Behavior

"Through our willingness to help others we can learn to be happy rather than depressed." – Gerald Jampolsky

Pillar #6: "Prosocial Behavior"

Helping others make us feel good. But did you know that doing good to others has significant physical and psychological benefits for you, the giver, as well?

A significant number of research studies have demonstrated that people who consistently help others, live healthier, happier lives — and may even live longer.

So it seems that a few little random acts of kindness on a regular basis go a long way to increasing your positive energy and overall quality of life.

Kindness, like other healthy lifestyle habits, doesn't just make other people happy; it improves your overall physical and emotional well-being.

For example, cardiac patients who regularly visit other cardiac in-patients to offer support, experience a heightened sense of purpose and reduced levels of despair and depression.

In addition, people who suffer from chronic pain have experienced decreased pain intensity, lower levels of disability, and less depression when they serve as peer volunteers for other chronic pain sufferers.

The power of volunteering was highlighted in yet another study by the Buck Center for Research in Aging. Researchers found that people fifty-five or older who volunteered for at least four hours each week had a forty-four percent lower likelihood of dying.

This implies that *volunteering is just as good for your health as exercising four days a week — or quitting smoking*.

What about kids and teens? Do the same benefits of kindness and volunteering apply to them too?

There is evidence that teens that volunteer enhance their self-esteem and social competence. Furthermore, volunteering helps to protect teens against anti-social behavior, substance abuse — and even helps to reduce teen pregnancies.

Some social scientists even believe that kids will develop better mental and physical health in adulthood if you teach them the power of kindness and volunteering at an early age.

Giving and the brain—The "helper's high"

Let's face it, doing good to others make us feel good; that's why we do it.

When we hold the door for someone, or help someone at the checkout counter when they don't have enough money, these unselfish acts of kindness that social scientists call "prosocial behavior" often leave us with a warm feeling.

This feeling we experience after giving aid to someone is often called "the helper's high."

But is this just a feeling, or is it the brain giving us feedback based on our actions?

As it turns out, researchers at the National Institute of Neurological Disorders and Stroke discovered, through FMR brain imaging, that making a charitable donation activated the same reward center in the brain (mesolimbic pathway) that is responsible for our experiencing pleasure through eating and sex.

Increase Your Prosocial Behaviour

In other words, we are hard-wired to help each other. It's in our DNA. When we help each other, the brain goes into a "dopamine-mediated euphoria" state that makes us feel good.

But would you also believe that just thinking about giving could lead to significant health benefits?

Harvard behavioral psychologist, David McClelland, discovered that students who watched a film of Mother Teresa taking care of orphans in Calcutta showed significant increases in the immune system antibody immunoglobulin A (S-IgA).

McClelland refer to this as the "Mother Teresa Effect."

Altruism in the workplace

Science has demonstrated again and again that kindness toward others causes us to be happier and healthier — with longer life spans.

So it should come as no surprise that people who enjoy helping their coworkers also tend to be more satisfied with their work. In a study published in the *Journal of Business Psychology*, researchers found that developing friendships at work increases organizational effectiveness and employee job satisfaction.

In short, organizations that create an environment of *camaraderie and a common sense of purpose, often experience higher productivity, increased employee job satisfaction, better employee retention*, and best of all, increased *profitability*.

7 Ways to Increase Your Positive Energy through Simple Acts of Kindness

1. Volunteer

At least once per month I volunteer at my daughters' kindergarten to assist the PE instructor. It's only an hour out of my day but it fills me up with positive energy from twenty little smiling faces.

What cause is worth your time?

2. Donate

Donating money to a worthy cause lights up the pleasure centers in the brain. So go ahead and contribute to a cause you believe in.

3. Hold the door for someone

Doesn't it make you feel good seeing how thankful someone is just because you held the door for him/her? Of course, it's not the physical act of holding the door that touches them, it's the fact that you cared enough. So be a gentleman or a lady, hold the door with a smile.

4. Have a conversation with a homeless person

You're likely thinking, "they're dirty and smelly." That's often true, but they're people just like you and me. And believe me, you're going to make that person's day, because by acknowledging them they feel seen. Can you imagine how terrible it must be to feel invisible in a crowded world? Sometimes, a few kind words are all it takes to shine a light on someone.

5. Compliment a stranger

We don't talk to each other anymore. In fact, we're so afraid of each other that we barely make eye contact — in the elevator, in the supermarket line, with our own neighbors. Don't live your life out of fear. Compliment someone tomorrow — on the way they dress, the perfume they're wearing, their colorful new shoes. Most importantly, be authentic and really mean what you say.

6. Acknowledge someone with a smile

How did you feel the last time a stranger smiled at you? I'm sure it felt pretty good, didn't it? A sincere smile is a simple and meaningful way of sharing positive energy with others. It's a nonverbal way of saying, "Hi, I see you and I hope you're having a great day."

7. Help a coworker who's having difficulties on the job

If a coworker is overwhelmed and you have time on your hands, why not offer to help? Be a team player. If someone is having difficulties with something you understand very well, why not share your expertise with them? Or simply offer to do some of their work so it can get done faster. The science is conclusive. When you help others at work it makes you happier and leads to a more satisfying work environment.

Prosocial Behavior Action Plan

Simple acts of kindness, good for the doer too.

1. How can you **make a difference** in someone else's life today with a **simpleact of kindness?**

Get Exclusive Extras at *EnergizedLifeAcademy.com*

~ **Energize Your Life Action Plan workbook**

~ **7 Questions (to Ask Yourself) to Help You
Fuel Your Life with Purpose, Passion & Play ebook**

~ **Free coaching videos on all seven pillars**

Give Yourself Permission to Play

*"We don't stop playing because we grow old;
We grow old because we stop playing."*
– George Bernard Shaw

Pillar #7: Play

When childhood dies, most of us become corpses of our younger selves.

We forget that it is through active play that we learn to navigate the world around us, adapt to the unexpected, and build lasting connections with others.

Without play, life becomes tedious, our relationships unsatisfying, and our work grinding and unfulfilling.

Can you imagine a world without art, books, movies, music, or comedy? This would be a world without creativity and imagination, where people focus solely on the demands of daily living.

Not a very exciting place to live, is it?

Without play, it is very difficult for us to connect with each other and build deep relationships.

Without play, we become rigid and set in our ways and are unable to adapt to the changing tides around us.

When we are play-deprived we tend to be unprepared to deal with the unexpected events of life. So we find it difficult to choose the appropriate emotional response for the situation.

Because the play-deprived individual is often rigid and has a limited repertoire of emotional responses, he often responds to surprises with fear, hostility, or withdrawal.

Play, after all, is what allows us to develop emotional resilience. Through our play, we're able to train our feelings and increase our capacity to respond appropriately to the unexpected.

Psychiatrist Stuart Brown, founder of The National Institute for Play, often compares play to oxygen. In his book, Play, he writes that like oxygen, "[play] is all around us; yet goes mostly unnoticed or unappreciated until it is missing."

Why Do Adults Need to Play?

We need to play because in our play we often find solutions to the problems that plague us.

Play takes us away from our everyday worries and responsibilities. It acts as a catalyst to boost creativity, improve productivity, and make our lives happier and better in every way.

Most importantly, when we play we often lose ourselves in the moment. These are moments of joy. And joy is one of the most energizing of the positive emotions. Joy moments, as I like to call them, leave smiles on our faces long after the activity has ended — or even when we recall what we did years later.

We need to play because as Barbara Brannen wrote in her book *The Gift of Play,*

> *"There is more for us to learn and know about ourselves hidden in our play. There is growth we have yet to go through, there are issues we have yet to deal with, and there are good times that are inside us dying to come out that haven't been given a chance."*

The Science of Play

In modern day society adult play is often perceived as unproductive or, at best, a guilty pleasure. After all, with so much on our plates, who has time to play?

Fortunately, over the past several decades scientists have begun to understand that play is a complex evolutionary mechanism that is crucial to social development, learning, creativity, positive emotions, and healthy aging.

In fact, the new science of epigenetics — that studies the changes in gene expression caused by environmental factors — has led scientists to the understanding that the human genome does not contain enough information to construct a fully social brain. Play and the many other basic emotional systems of several regions of the brain are the tools that allow the social brain to develop.

Furthermore, scientists have discovered that the same regions of the brain — the nucleus accumbens, amygdala, and frontal cortex — responsible for pleasure, motivation, and positive emotions, are also the areas of the brain that regulate play.

What does this tell us?

It tells us that at our core, the drive to *play is as important to the human animal as food and sex.* It's how we learn. In fact, optimal brain development depends on healthy play experiences in early life. And as we grow older, play helps to nourish *social learning,* enhance *creative problem-solving* skills, and provide a healthy dose of *positive emotions.*

The Brain on Play

A 2003 study coauthored by Washington State University neuroscientist Jaak Panksepp, reported that play promotes neural development in the "higher" brain areas involved in emotional reactions and social learning.

In the study, researchers discovered that play released a protein called brain-derived neurotrophic factor (BDNF), that stimulates the growth of new neurons. Neurons are nerve cells that allow the brain to communicate with the rest of your body and the outside environment.

Other studies have also clearly demonstrated that *play fosters creative thinking in children and adults*.

Play and On The Job Productivity

Those of us who spend a lot of time with young kids quickly come to realize that their little minds are filled with out-of-the-box creative ideas. Why are they able to generate these off-the-wall ideas? They spend most of their days at play.

Today some of the most innovative companies such as Google, Southwest Airlines, Cartoon Network, and others, have realized that the marriage of work and play makes for more creative and productive employees.

Unfortunately, having fun at work is not the norm for most companies, but it should be. Several studies have demonstrated that having fun in the workplace does boost employee productivity, morale, creativity, and loyalty.

For example, one such study from the University of Florida reported that having fun at work increases employees' job engagement, performance, and teamwork.

7 Ways to Increase Your Positive Energy through Play

*"A lack of play should be treated like malnutrition –
it's a health risk to your body and mind."* – Stuart Brown, M.D.

1. Give yourself permission to play

The most important thing to remember is that play is a state of mind. You don't have to be a practical joker, closet comedian, or a goofball to enjoy the benefits of a playful life. However, you must grant yourself permission to loosen up and start seeing the world through the lenses of your playful inner child.

A simple place to start is to *allow yourself to do something that is totally uncharacteristic* of you. Tell a joke, wear a crazy hat or jacket, talk to your dog, smile at a stranger.

What you do is up to you, but give yourself permission to break out of your serious adult role and just be a kid again.

2. Find Your "Heart Play"

In her book *The Gift of Play* Barbara Brannen wrote, "Heart Play makes your heart sing and fly free." She said it involves no unwelcome work, nor does it come with any responsibility. In fact, your "Heart Play" creates "an ecstasy that may not be apparent to anyone but you."

When was the last time you just let loose and let your heart sing? Yes, I know, we've all been conditioned by society to play our roles. I'm an attorney. I'm a doctor. I'm an executive. I'm a professional. I'm a responsible grown-up.

But is that who you really are? What would that little kid inside of you jump out and start doing if you were to break the adult chain that keeps him or her a prisoner under your own skin?

What made your heart sing before you assumed the (adult) role of being the walking stiff? Yes, remember. Go there.

You may have to go way back to your childhood to rediscover your Heart Play, but it's buried in there somewhere. Even if your childhood was completely play-deprived, deep down there are things you wished you could have experienced.

So what is your unique way of playing when no one is watching — and judging you? Get out your shovel and dig, dig, dig until you find your own lost treasure.

For me, my heart sings whenever I participate in improvisational dancing. Or get me on the dance floor with some old Afro-Cuban Mambo music and a partner who's able to just let go and my untamed spirit lets loose!

What else gives me this feeling of "dancing with God," as I called it in my book *Fitness & Spirituality?*

Give Yourself Permission to Play

Running in the Santa Monica mountains overlooking the ocean at dawn; roller-dancing at Venice Beach; rollerblading along the ocean bike path from Venice to Santa Monica on a hot summer day listening to Terence Trent Darby; playing a great game of tennis; and of course, skiing from the top of Mammoth mountain on a clear day with fresh powder.

So, what makes your heart sing?

Is it gardening, playing cards, board games, reading, playing an instrument, golf, playing with your dog, hiking, good conversation with old friends?

Your Heart Play is whatever you do that leaves you thinking to yourself, "I wish this moment would last forever." It leaves you with a feeling of joy.

And as Barbara Brannen so eloquently puts it...

> *"Joy is that wonderfully mysterious feeling that warms our souls,*
> *puts an involuntary smile on our faces and causes the heart to*
> *pump our blood in a way that nourishes our body."*

Your Heart Play will lead to a feeling of joy. And joy, along with all the other positive emotions, will energize your life and make you feel alive.

3. Claim Your "Joy Moments"

I wrote earlier that play brings joy. Joy is also the feeling that automatically puts a smile on your face when you recall past moments of play.

But in order to claim these "joy moments," as I like to call them, we have to force ourselves to play again. We have to learn to laugh and be silly. To follow our spontaneous urges, to let loose and skip like a child. Never mind that you're wearing a business suit.

The funny thing is when you give yourself permission to play others around you will automatically give themselves permission to play as well.

Play, like laughter, is contagious.

Speaking of laughter, when was the last time you watched a really funny movie or stand-up act that was so outrageous it made you laugh until you cried? I still laugh when I think about scenes from Richard Pryor in concert, or movies like Borat, The Hangover, Airplane, and Monty Python.

A good "belly laugh" will lead to many of these joy moments.

Another of my favorite play activities is tickling my daughter on the floor. She gets so into it that before long we're both laughing and rolling around playing other games.

This is what happens when you allow yourself to experience the joy of spontaneous play; it often leads to other activities that enhance your positive emotions.

So go ahead, give yourself permission to get in touch with your playful inner kid. Play not only gets you in touch with your joy moments, it also clears your thinking and gives you a well needed energy boost.

As Barbara Brannen puts it in The Gift of Play:

> *"Play is an energy boost without the energy bar or energy drink."*

4. Steal a few "play moments" each day

Play is all around us, but is generally only noticed by the playful at heart. You stand in a line at the supermarket, post office, bank, or airport. Why not use this as an opportunity to increase your play quota for the day.

You don't have to be a comedian. You just have to be open to the opportunities that present themselves.

For instance, just last week I was at the supermarket and the checkout line was very long. This was obviously very irritating for the lady in front of me because at one point she threw her arms up and said, "I'm never coming here again."

Sensing the opportunity to change the energy dynamic I playfully responded, "Are you kidding me, I met my wife in this very line."

Of course that wasn't the case, but it got a laugh and got everybody in line smiling and talking to each other. Did I feel better about my shopping experience than if I had adopted her negative attitude? You bet! And I imagine she did too.

So just by adapting a playful attitude about life, not only will you be open to more play opportunities, but you can also create a shift in the energy dynamic of your circumstances and thus change life's little annoyances into energizing play moments.

If you're a parent, another area where you can steal little play moments is with your kids. Just a few minutes ago as I sat at my desk writing, my daughter walked up to me (for the third time in the past fifteen minutes) and in her cute little voice said, "Daddy, can I play with you?"

But this time, before I could reply with my usual, "Not now, honey, I'll play with you when I'm done here," she reached out with her little palm and gently turned my head towards her and gave me the biggest kiss, with sound affects (MUAAAAH), the way she often does when she really wants something.

Now how could I possibly say no to that? The bottom line is we proceeded to have a great time playing with memory game cards and laughing at her many attempts to cheat.

That was a special play moment — that turned into another of my many joy moments — that will put a smile on my face every time I read this chapter of the book.

So remember, play opportunities are all around you. And all you have to do to steal a few play moments each day is to adapt a playful attitude.

A five or ten minute play break could reward you with a clear head and a new perspective on whatever task you're working on.

So go ahead; *be a thief. Steal a few play moments each day.* You'll be rewarded with the gift of feeling energized and alive again.

5. Practice your "play signals"

Have you ever wondered how animals know that an approaching animal is looking to play and not attack them?

They send "play signals" to each other.

If you watch a dog who wants to play with another, he gets very excited, wags his tail rapidly, and most often used the "play bow" (the front-down-rear-up posture) as an invitation to play.

Like animals, people use play signals too. We often don't recognize the signals because most of the time when we meet people — on elevators, subways, or walking by — we're too afraid of what an interaction might bring.

So we've conditioned ourselves over the years to practice what social scientists call "avoidant behaviors." We stare at a spot on the wall, fiddle with our phones, or do anything we can to look busy.

Animals also use play signals to communicate with each other that they're not a threat. They just want to play. Humans do the same thing too.

When we smile and look folks in the eyes without staring, we're in essence inviting them to reciprocate our gesture and participate in the first stage of a bonding ritual.

We may even attempt to make small talk — commenting on the weather, or paying a complement.

These are all play signals that say to the other person, "I'm not a threat, I just want to play and see where it goes."

It may go nowhere or it may change your life forever. Either way you will never know unless you get over the fear of what such interactions may bring.

When you practice sending play signals, some people will respond and others won't. Either way, that's fine. Eventually you will make connections with other fun-loving people, if even for an instant.

Sending play signals often will help you steal some of those simple "play moments" that enhance your positive emotions and brighten up your day.

6. Be aware of "play killers"

Play is a habit that has to be nurtured. You have to get out there and practice regularly and eventually you will find the right kind of play for you that nourish your soul.

But like "energy suckers," that I wrote about in an earlier chapter (whose presence sucks the life out of you and leaves you drained like a wilted plant) "play killers" will also attempt to steal your joy.

A play killer might be a well-meaning parent, or an insecure spouse. He or she might even be your best girlfriend or buddy. How can you tell?

If someone doesn't understand, appreciate, or respect your need for play then he or she might be a "play killer." You might even find yourself in situations or relationships that are oppressive or abusive. That, too, is a "play killer."

As psychiatrist Stuart Brown wrote in his book *Play,*

> *"Part of nourishing your play is putting yourself in an environment that supports and promotes that play."*

So if you don't feel play-nourished by the people around you, change your environment. Go out and find others who understand and support your need to play.

7. "Play together" in your personal relationships

Couples that play together stay together. Or should I say they're more likely to stay together. After all, who would you rather be with, someone you're having fun with, or someone who bores you to death.

Let's face it; if you've been in a relationship with someone for a while, the romance will eventually fade. It doesn't have to disappear, but there most likely won't be the same passionate, sexual attraction that brought you together in the first place. And this is natural.

Some experts believe that there are various systems in the human brain that correspond to different levels of love.

Erotic love has evolved to help us attract others and find a mate. Romantic love helps us to focus our energies on staying with that mate once we find him or her. And the highest stage of love is what some experts refer to as attachment.

Relationship experts theorize that the attachment phase of love has evolved over time to keep two people together long enough to raise children — even after the passion and romance fades away.

However, a number of research studies have confirmed that couples that play and have fun together are generally happier in their relationships.

One such study from the University of Denver developed a fun and friendship scale to rate couple's relationship satisfaction. The couples that regularly made time for fun and getting to know each other on a deeper level scored the highest.

Another study published in the *Journal of Personality and Social Psychology* by psychologist Arthur Aron of State University of New York-Stony Brook, found that the couples that engaged in *new, unfamiliar and playful* activities had the highest relationship satisfaction scores.

Of course, we really don't need research to tell us that playing together leads to higher satisfaction in a relationship. But the science is clear that play increases the level of dopamine in the brain. Dopamine is a hormone and neurotransmitter — a chemical released by nerve cells to send signals to other nerve cells — that plays a major role in the brain's pleasure and reward system.

Through his case studies and "play histories" with couples, psychiatrist Stuart Brown also discovered that:

> *"The defining factor among couples who were able to find romance again, and even to find new fields of emotional intimacy previously unexplored, was that they were able to find ways to play together. Those who played together, stayed together. Those who didn't either split or, worse yet, simply endured an unhappy and dysfunctional relationship."*

Remember, play leads to joy and joy is one of the most powerful of the positive emotions. So, couples that play together will more likely experience more joy in their relationship.

And *joy is a fuel for love*.

Play Action Plan

Play increases our capacity to respond appropriately to the unexpected.

1. What is your "Heart Play?"
2. How can you steal a few play moments today?
3. What new fun and unfamiliar activity can you and your spouse/significant other engage in today, this week, or this month?

Closing Note: Every Energy Reaction Needs a Catalyst, What's Yours?

Would you believe that an average human body contains enough stored energy to fill a one-ton battery? So obviously, we do not lack energy. What we often lack is the ability to access the many sources of energy that are available to us.

We're not going to feel physically energized by sitting on our butts all day. Such a sedentary lifestyle is contrary to the laws of energy. For one thing, a body at rest contains an abundance of "potential" or stored energy. But in order to use that energy, we have to first find a way to set that body into motion.

This requires some form of "activation energy." In chemistry, activation energy is the minimum amount of energy required to speed up a reaction. So if your body is at rest it's going to take some amount of activation energy — in the form of movement — to make you feel energized and alive.

Activation energy is usually supplied by a "catalyst." Physically, your catalyst can be any form of movement or exercise. This helps you to access the energy of physical vitality.

Each of the seven pillars will require a different catalyst. For example, making the decision to either find ways to love your job or make a plan to leave it is a catalyst that will energize your life beyond measure. *Because passion energizes and purpose motivates*. So the pursuit of fulfillment and meaning is a powerful catalyst that ignites passion and purpose to fuel our lives.

Cultivating positive energy is a daily practice. It requires some effort on our part. It's also a choice. Like love, it is up to us to choose to live a happy, playful, and meaningful life. It won't happen unless we choose it.

So why not choose to live and work with passion and purpose, accelerate your *personal evolution,* cultivate physical vitality, become a conduit for *positive energy,* practice *positive psychology,* increase your *prosocial behavior,* and give yourself *permission to play?*

To make this choice is to unleash the energy that lays dormant within, and to choose LIFE: Living In Full Expression.

Making the choice to live an energized life is a choice to learn to "enjoy and find meaning in the ... process of living itself," as Mihaly Csikszentmihalyi puts it.

In short, to live an energized life is to come alive. It is to choose the road less traveled. It is to live as Wilfred Petterson, author of The Art of Living, suggested:

> *"Walk with the dreamers*
> *the believers*
> *the courageous*
> *the cheerful*
> *the planners*
> *the doers*
> *the successful people with their heads in the clouds*
> *and their feet on the ground*
> *let their spirit ignite a fire within you*
> *to leave this world better than when you found it."*

Remember, we are only on this earth for a very short time, so why not ignite your fire, energize your life and come alive?

You can make a difference. The world needs what you've got!

Get Exclusive Extras at *EnergizedLifeAcademy.com*

~ **Energize Your Life Action Plan workbook**

~ **7 Questions (to Ask Yourself) to Help You
Fuel Your Life with Purpose, Passion & Play ebook**

~ **Free coaching videos on all seven pillars**

Energize Your Life Tools & Resources

About The Author

Del Millers (aka Dr. Del) started his career as an Electrical Engineer and Pharmaceutical Sales Rep for some of the top Fortune 500 companies in corporate America. After four years in corporate America, however, he made the discovery that he is not the employee type. So he hung up his suit and tie and bid farewell to corporate America to pursue the uncertain life of an entrepreneur.

Dr. Del has since authored eight books on nutrition, fitness, and personal growth. Through his online training courses — The Best You Academy and Energized Life Academy — Dr. Del has consulted with clients on four continents and in six different countries on how to fuel their lives and work with positive energy, and find freedom, fulfillment, and fun.

Dr. Del has a PhD in Nutritional Sciences and a Masters degree in psychology. He lives in Los Angeles, California with his wife and three daughters.

Essential Reading:

1. Flow: The psychology of optimal experience, by Mihaly Csikszentmihalyi
2. How to Find Fulfilling Work, by Roman Krznaric
3. Turn Your Passion into Profit, by Walt Goodridge
4. Start with Why, by Simon Sinek
5. The Science of Getting Rich, by Wallace Wattles
6. The Energy Addict & The Energy Bus, by Jon Gordon
7. Drive: The surprising truth about what motivates us, by Daniel Pink
8. Learned Optimism, by Martin Seligman
9. Play, by Stuart Brown
10. The Gift of Play, by Barbara Brannen
11. The Art of Living, by Wilfred Petterson
12. The Power of Full Engagement by Jim Loehr and Tony Schwartz
13. Are You Fully Charged? by Tom Rath
14. Screw Work Let's Play, by John Williams

Books by Dr. Del:

1. Fitness & Spirituality: How to Make the Connection
2. Dr. Del's 10-Minute Meals
3. Dr. Del's Rapid Fatloss Manual
4. Dr. Del's Rapid Fatloss Meal Plan
5. Dr. Del's Rapid Fatloss Cookbook
6. Dr. Del's Rapid Fatloss Detox-Cleanse Program

Dr. Del's Online Training Courses:

The Best You Academy:
Expand Your Energy Capacity and Energize Your Lifestyle
TheBestYouAcademy.com

Get These Exclusive Extras Free:
- 7 Simple Ways to Expand Your Energy Capacity and Energize Your Lifestyle ebook
- Free coaching videos

Energized Life Academy:
Design a Life of Purpose, Passion & Play
EnergizedLifeAcademy.com

Get These Exclusive Extras Free:
- Energize Your Life Action Plan Workbook
- 7 Questions (to Ask Yourself) to Help You Fuel Your Life with Purpose, Passion & Play ebook
- Free coachng videos on all seven pillars

Connect with Dr. Del:

Facebook.com/drdelmillers

Twitter.com/drdelmillers

Youtube.com/drdelmillers

LinkedIn.com/in/drdelmillers

Pinterest.com/drdelmillers

Dr. Del's Weekly Blog & Podcasts

www.drdelmillers.com

www.ingramcontent.com/pod-product-compliance
Lightning Source LLC
Chambersburg PA
CBHW031601110426
42742CB00036B/575